PRAISE FOR GORDON DAUGHERTY
AND *STARTUP SUCCESS*

"Gordon has a way of explaining complex fundraising topics very clearly and in ways that are actionable."

—GREGG ALVAREZ

"As we move along the path towards a Series A, Gordon is giving incredibly concrete advice that we can actually act on. This is huge for us."

—TONY NASH

"Whether you're a first-time founder or have already raised millions from VCs, *Startup Success* is a book you want close by before hitting the fundraising trail! What makes this book really shine is Daugherty's pragmatic advice on the process of running a successful fundraising campaign."

—ANDY O'HARA, Founder & CEO, Chiron Health

"Daugherty does an incredible job deconstructing an otherwise stressful and unfamiliar process."

—YOUSEF KASSIM, Founder & CEO, Easy Expunctions

"*Startup Success* is so actionable that I immediately started applying the concepts as I read. Now I know not only exactly where I stand in the process, but also how much energy and focus I should spend at each stage."

—**RAMON BERRIOS**, CEO, Trend

"I meet lots of founders who don't fully understand fundraising strategy and best practices. They should read *Startup Success* before pitching VCs. One of Gordon's superpowers is explaining complex fundraising topics very clearly."

—**KELSI KAMIN**, Venture Capital Investor

"An entrepreneur will reference this book many times as they develop different lenses of their entrepreneurial journey."

—**LISA MCCOMB**, Founder & CEO, Rectify

"This book does an excellent job of taking all of Gordon's words of wisdom and communicating them in a way that is useful to any entrepreneur."

—**DAVID ZAKARIAIE**, Founder & CEO, Senseye

STARTUP

SUCCESS

GORDON DAUGHERTY

RIVER GROVE
BOOKS

This publication is designed to provide accurate and authoritative information in regard to the subject matter covered. It is sold with the understanding that the publisher and author are not engaged in rendering legal, accounting, or other professional services. Nothing herein shall create an attorney-client relationship, and nothing herein shall constitute legal advice or a solicitation to offer legal advice. If legal advice or other expert assistance is required, the services of a competent professional should be sought.

Published by River Grove Books
Austin, TX
www.rivergrovebooks.com

Distributed by River Grove Books

Design and composition by Greenleaf Book Group
Cover design by Greenleaf Book Group
Cover images used under license from ©Shutterstock.com/shymar27;
©Shutterstock.com/Jacky Co; ©Shutterstock.com/Ljupco Smokovski;
©Shutterstock.com/lucadp

Publisher's Cataloging-in-Publication data is available.

Print ISBN: 978-1-63299-245-1

eBook ISBN: 978-1-63299-246-8

First Edition

"The best time to plant a tree was 20 years ago; the next best time is today."

—Chinese proverb

CONTENTS

Foreword ix

Preface xi

Acknowledgments xiii

Introduction 1

Chapter 1: Setting the Stage 7

Chapter 2: Fundraising Strategy 29

Chapter 3: Planning Your Campaign 47

Chapter 4: Your Fundraising Toolkit 67

Chapter 5: Demystifying Convertible Securities . . .99

Chapter 6: The Seed Fundraising Dance 119

Chapter 7: Series A Fundraising 135

Chapter 8: Interacting with Investors 159

Chapter 9: Negotiating Valuation 189

Closing Thoughts 211

Index 213

About the Author 223

FOREWORD

I started my career from my college dorm room during the first dot-com boom with an Internet startup. Since then, I've been a founder, a CEO, a mentor, an angel investor, and a venture capitalist. I've raised millions of dollars, made millions of dollars, and invested millions of dollars. Now I'm one of the most active early-stage tech investors in Texas. I've worked with thousands of entrepreneurs along the way.

I've been fortunate to be on the same side of the table as Gordon for the past seven years during most of those deals. We've invested together, solved problems together, and watched our "babies grow up" from seed-stage investments to approaching IPO. We saw more startups during that time than most investors do because of our unique investment strategy, and because of this, Gordon's pool of experience is even wider and deeper than you would expect, given his already extensive and successful business background.

Before I met him, Gordon had a few careers' worth of experience as an executive and entrepreneur in the driver's seat. He's an operator who knows how to do the work himself and also how to build and manage high-performance teams. He knows how important people are and takes the time to invest in them individually. He has taught me a lot about being a great husband and father—and that isn't in his Capital Factory job description.

I've had the chance to see how Gordon works and how he makes decisions for himself, for his family, and for the entrepreneurs he advises. He knows what he doesn't know and doesn't speak up until he has something important to say. When he does speak up, everyone has learned it's a good idea to listen carefully.

Gordon has always had a passion for mentorship and teaching others—that's the thing that brought us together from the beginning. Gordon has been developing content and honing his skills for decades. I've seen him give dozens of lectures, mentor hundreds of entrepreneurs, and help navigate some really sticky situations. He now spends the majority of his time doing that—mentoring entrepreneurs and serving as an advisor or board member.

His passion for educating shines through, and he does it in a way that lifts other people up and makes them feel empowered. Gordon has a way of explaining things in simple terms that makes intimidating topics more accessible. If you're part of the Capital Factory portfolio, you get to work with him in person and receive personalized, one-on-one advice. If you're not, this book is your next best way to get inside his head and transfer his wealth of experience to your own. Be sure to check out his online video series as well!

In this book, Gordon walks you through a fundraising campaign and ultimate negotiation—step-by-step. You'll get your head in the game, come up with a strategy, plan and execute a campaign, and then negotiate a deal. Read it. Put it to practice. Read it again.

Joshua Baer
Founder & CEO, Capital Factory
Austin, Texas
August 2019

PREFACE

Going back about 20 years ago, if I discovered that I gave out the same piece of advice more than once in a short period of time, I would just write it down. With that, the next time it happened, I could just email the document and then answer any remaining questions or adapt it to a specific situation. That continued until I decided to organize and publish the documents on a blog (ShockwaveInnovations.com). Advising and investing in startups along the way triggered lots more articles, and I found that I truly enjoyed figuring out what it was that I knew, or thought I knew, and whether I could communicate it both in written form and in such a way that others could understand it and take action accordingly. Getting feedback from founders about how much they were helped and how easy my articles were to understand really fueled me to continue writing.

One day, I realized I had published more than 150 articles, produced 50 streaming videos, personally helped several hundred entrepreneurs, and been involved in making more than 200 early-stage investments as a venture capitalist and angel investor. I've also had some hand in raising more than $80 million in growth and venture capital, either as an executive operator or as an active advisor.

One of my greatest pleasures came one day when I was doing mentor office hours with a founder. She had an ear-to-ear grin on her face when she said, "This weekend, I binge-read your whole blog, and it's fabulous. There is so much I want to talk to you about today." At the end of our meeting, she asked, "Have you ever thought about writing a book?"

Hmmm, interesting idea.

ACKNOWLEDGMENTS

This book could not have been completed without the support of many people, including the following:

My wife and best friend, Kelly, who has lovingly supported so many of my crazy and ambitious endeavors during our more than 25 years together.

My mother and father, who raised me with a set of ethics and principles that guide me to this day and inspired me to write my own book, just as they did as a writer-producer duo when I was young.

My daughters, Kirra, Kayla, and Meagan, who make me proud every day as they make their own marks on this world in which we live—one that will benefit greatly as more women achieve deserved leadership positions in both business and government.

Joel Trammell, Joshua Baer, Mellie Price, and Mikey Trafton, who taught me so much about what it means to be a real entrepreneur and who serve as role models to so many others.

I must thank the startups I've worked with for entrusting me with advisory and board director roles and for letting me selfishly learn about new industries, technologies, and business models; I hope I've helped them a little along the way.

Hundreds of startups have participated in the Capital Factory accelerator program since late 2012, when I took it on as my baby and have tried to nurture it ever since. Their questions and pursuit of advice have helped me more completely discover what it is that I actually know. I could not have written this book without that.

INTRODUCTION

I n this day and age, it takes almost nothing to start a startup. After some coffee shop meetings with an equally passionate co-founder, you discover that you have a lot of ideas, an outline of a business plan, and a willingness to spend nights and weekends doing really hard work. Congratulations; you've got yourself a startup.

It also takes very little funding capital for most types of startup ventures to reach interesting milestones of achievement. Decades ago, we had to raise millions of dollars just to get a v1.0 software product built and only then discover whether the world suffered enough from a particular problem to actually pay to have it solved. Today, due to things like open-source software, inexpensive hosting services, and coworking spaces, we can often achieve those same initial milestones by spending only tens or hundreds of thousands of dollars.

Although this book is all about funding the early stages of your venture, the amount of money you raise over time should not be your measure of success—building a great company is. In fact, you might ultimately decide that you don't want or need to raise money for your startup venture in order to achieve your goals. That is perfectly OK. When you hear other entrepreneurs brag about how much money they've raised instead of bragging about how many happy, paying customers they have or how much revenue they've generated, don't mimic their behavior. In fact, the definition of *great company* doesn't even have to mean huge or with a unicorn valuation. Instead, it can mean having a significant social impact or employing 50 people who are all passionate about solving a particular problem and absolutely love working for your company. Many startups never reach even $10 million in revenues, but that doesn't mean they can't become sustainable and provide satisfaction and value to their founders, employees, and customers.

Fundraising is a personal choice. It's one that is sometimes driven by *want* and other times by *need*. There is also a choice of when to first raise funding from external sources. Injections of funding do typically cause a business to grow faster and accomplish more in a given period of time. But with that comes a new set of obligations and accountability—to the investors that provided the capital. Some founders choose to delay that until they've at least built their product and gained paying customers, whereas other founders decide to take on funding earlier. Again, it's a personal choice. This book will help you make your own decisions about fundraising over time. So, as you read about the various stages of fundraising and their associated attributes and recommended best practices, don't interpret that as a requirement for pursuing the same path; the choice is yours.

You will quickly learn that your most valuable resource is actually time (i.e., runway). Think of it like an hourglass. When the last grains of sand drop from the top to the bottom, you have to pack up your toys and go home. The game is over. Fundraising is one way to flip the hourglass over to gain more time, but not the only way. So are crowdfunding presales, government grants, and even large customer contracts with an up-front payment. With enough time, you can adjust and adapt until you eventually build a great team and identify a viable business model that enables you to become sustainable and—hopefully—also scalable.

With this focus on optimizing for time comes the development of unbelievable survival strengths and the ability to stare at a diminishing bank account without totally freaking out. You will get good at both throwing and catching Hail Mary passes while maintaining a smile on your face and a spring in your step, so that investors and others conclude that you and your business venture are both amazing.

I will describe this book by first telling you what it is not. It is not a cookbook, but it certainly includes many ingredients for success. It is not a step-by-step guide, but it is organized based on a logical sequence of events. It is also not a reference guide for every possible fundraising legal term or for fully decoding an investment term sheet. Rather, I decided to write something different that best exploits the gray in my hair and the hard lessons I've learned.

My personal goal is to help you best plan for and navigate the fundraising journey while also helping make sense of the regular chaos and frustrations you will face (or are already facing) during the process. Said a different way, I want to deliver you a long list of valuable insights and genuine aha moments that will dramatically improve your odds of fundraising success.

Most of the concepts in this book are written from the perspective of funding an early-stage technology venture, and many of the examples you will see are for a subscription software company. But don't let that distract or discourage you if you're building a different type of business. Most of the described concepts and best practices apply to early-stage ventures of all types—hardware, services, consumer packaged goods (CPG), and more.

Armed with this new knowledge that gets supplemented with progressive experience as you embark on your fundraising journey, you will quickly realize there is no single scenario that is perfect. There are best practices for certain aspects of the fundraising journey, and that is the focus of this book. Rounds of funding involve multiple players with respective motivations and personalities, trade-offs of risk and reward, and plenty of legal terms. The combinations are endless. Your mission is not to find the perfect scenario but rather a reasonable one that lets you continue the pursuit of your vision.

The chapters that follow represent numerous fundraising insights, tips, hints, and tricks I've discovered and refined over my professional career from the hundreds of early-stage investments I've been involved in making as an investor and from more than 19 years of mentoring and advising tons of startup founders. Some of the concepts you'll learn about are unique, whereas others are established best practices. You will also learn about numerous tools that will help minimize the chaos and streamline the time frame for getting funded. I hope you find the information in the pages that follow enlightening, actionable, and encouraging.

Let's find some of those aha moments together. And best of luck starting and building a great company!

CHAPTER 1

SETTING THE STAGE

*"I never failed once. It just happened to
be a 2,000-step process."*

—Thomas Edison

Since you turned the page from the introduction, I am assuming that you have either decided to raise outside funding for your venture or you first want to learn more about the whole process so that you can make that determination. But since I don't know your current starting point, let's just start at the beginning.

BOOTSTRAPPING

With as little as it costs to get a software startup off the ground these days, many entrepreneurs start off as *bootstrappers* rather than fundraisers. Bootstrapping is when your company supports itself on existing or personally available resources rather than external sources of capital. Many startup ventures are initially bootstrapped until a sufficient business plan is developed and some minimal level of validation exists in order to attract investors. There's nothing wrong with bootstrapping, but staying in that mode for too long can carry some consequences that you should understand if you're just getting started and later plan to raise money from investors.

There are many different methods of bootstrapping. For example, living off your savings account so you can work full-time on your startup venture is bootstrapping. Borrowing against your 401(k) retirement account to pay your bills while working full-time on your startup venture will cause you to incur debt and might not be recommended by your financial advisor, but it is bootstrapping. Working on your startup venture during nights and weekends while funding it with income from a day job is bootstrapping. Selling your car, leasing out your garage apartment, and auctioning off your valuable comic book collection to pay for your business expenses is bootstrapping. Secretly selling your spouse's car and auctioning off his sentimental family heirloom paintings might cause a divorce, but if you use the proceeds to fund your venture, it is bootstrapping. Convincing others to work on your venture for no cash compensation while combining with any of the previous options is badass ninja bootstrapping.

What about investing your own capital to fund the engineering work to build a prototype of the product? That's *not* bootstrapping; it's self-funding.

What about friends and family funding? Borrowing money from Aunt Sally and Uncle Fred or convincing some sorority sisters to make a small investment to help you out *is not* bootstrapping. Instead, it's an external investment just like borrowing money from a bank or convincing an investor to write a check. I mention this because I often hear entrepreneurs brag about bootstrapping all the way to their product launch, only to later discover prior investments from friends and family. I tip my hat to their accomplishment and then inform them about my definition of bootstrapping.

OK, you get the idea. It's less important to have an official definition than it is to evaluate and understand the commonalities among the various methods and approaches to bootstrapping. We often refer to bootstrapped ventures and bootstrap-minded founders as *scrappy*. There are definitely benefits of being scrappy in the early days while you're still trying to figure things out. But there are downsides that need to be understood as well, especially if the bootstrapping continues for a long period of time.

BENEFITS OF BOOTSTRAPPING

Many of the successful entrepreneurs that I respect the most are consummate and repeat bootstrappers. In fact, they take great pride in letting you know they're bootstrappers. If you look, you'll find them in your own community.

Before we talk about how long to bootstrap, let's review some of the biggest benefits of bootstrapping. Some of you will be able to skip the bootstrap phase altogether for one reason or another, and that's great. But you'll miss out on at least some of the benefits.

Bootstrapping forces founders to find and attract other team members that have genuine passion for the problem being solved versus those looking for a paycheck. It causes hyper-focus on making rapid and sufficient progress to either be able to get funded or start bringing in revenue from product sales. It forces a detailed understanding of exactly where every dollar is being spent and its specific value to the mission.

Bootstrapping fosters maximum creativity, flexibility, and instincts for survival. It avoids investors telling you what to do, giving you a hard time about the decisions you're making, or asking for a bunch of updates. Future investor prospects will be impressed by your passion and personal commitment to the venture as evidenced by your bootstrapping phase.

It is also true that a phase of bootstrapping comes with no dilution. In other words, you and your co-founders get to divvy up 100% of the equity. But there's a reason that I mention the dilution benefit last. Please don't extend your bootstrap phase as long as possible just to avoid dilution. If your business venture is best developed and grown by taking on some investment, you will be happier and richer in the long run if you do so. One of my favorite sayings is "Optimize for growth, not dilution." You would much rather have a single-digit equity stake in a venture that eventually exits via acquisition or IPO at a valuation of $1 billion than having double-digit equity in a venture that crashes and burns or exits for $2 million, $10 million, or even $50 million.

DEFINITION: DILUTION

Dilution is the result of an activity that causes a shareholder's equity to be reduced (diluted). Since equity is calculated by dividing a shareholder's quantity of shares by the total shares held by the company, the most common causes of dilution involve issuing additional shares of stock into the company. This could happen as a result of raising an equity round of funding or needing to create a new stock option pool with available shares of stock. In both cases, the number of issued shares increases, and this causes each of the previous shareholders' equity positions to be diluted.

HOW LONG SHOULD YOU BOOTSTRAP?

To answer this question, I need to set aside ventures that are planned to organically become profitable and sustainable on their own. Instead, I want to describe the more traditional tech startup scenario of pursuing multiple rounds of funding over time to grow aggressively and eventually reach a big exit.

I usually recommend bootstrapping at least long enough to gain sufficient evidence that your solution is desirable, which means your target customer wants it bad enough that they're willing to pay for it. It's also beneficial if you're able to prove that the solution idea is feasible, which means it can be built to deliver the intended benefit. That doesn't necessarily mean you will end up with a v1.0 product ready to launch after the bootstrapping phase, but rather that you should have enough proof that there's minimal technical risk.

With both desirability and feasibility validated (or mostly validated), you still have a long way to go before you've grown a great company that's both scalable and sustainable, as you can see from figure 1.1, but you are considerably less risky than before desirability and feasibility were validated. And that means you could be ready to pursue a round of funding. There are dozens of reasons why you still might not be successful getting funded, but that's a topic for a future chapter.

Most startups that follow this approach will raise their first round of funding to launch the product and seek hints or proof of viability. Viability means the customer acquisition model yields a customer lifetime value (LTV) that is greater than the customer acquisition cost (CAC). Not just a little greater, but sufficiently greater to cover the costs of the other functions that aren't related to customer acquisition, as well as various other operational overhead.

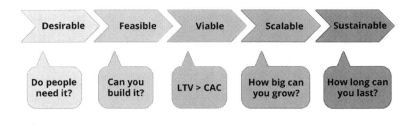

Figure 1.1. Levels of startup viability

THE DANGERS OF BOOTSTRAPPING TOO LONG

From time to time I come across startups that have been in boot-strap mode for a seemingly long time. You might be thinking that with all of the bootstrapping benefits I listed earlier, why not stay in this mode as long as possible? There are a few reasons to consider if you plan to raise funding from investors.

SLOW PROGRESS FOR TOO LONG

While in bootstrap mode, your financial resources are limited enough that your progress is also limited. If that goes on too long, investors might ask, "How is it that you've been working on this for almost two and a half years and only have ___ customers and

___ revenue?" Investors like to connect many dots, but when they connect yours over a long period of time, the slope of the curve isn't very interesting.

MINDSET

The processes, culture, and general mindset of bootstrappers is fairly different from those that are funded and dialing in a big outcome. Staying in the bootstrap mode too long can cause that mindset to sink in to the point that investors are forced to wonder if you'll be able to shift multiple gears directly into a big-outcome mentality after getting funded.

ASSUMPTIONS

Investors can easily assume your business venture went through a significant pivot, multiple pivots, a co-founder breakup, unsuccessful prior fundraising attempts, and so on. It's even possible that some of those things are exactly true and caused the bootstrap phase to last longer than intended. But investors will often pile on additional negative or skeptical assumptions—overshadowing whatever you choose to reveal. They might assume the market is too small or doesn't sufficiently suffer from the stated problem. Or they might even assume you're not the right team to grow a successful company.

As I hope you've concluded, bootstrapping during the early days, until you've mostly demonstrated desirability and feasibility for your business venture, can be a great thing. But too much of a great thing can turn into a bad thing.

Compare notes with your co-founders and trusted advisors so you have a general strategy and plan for your bootstrap phase. Once you're ready to take on your first round of investment, prepare for a change in mentality. You will have obligations and accountability to outsiders—namely your investors.

WHAT'S IN A NAME, ANYWAY?

The name of a round of funding is often used to describe the evolutionary phase of a startup. If I told you about a startup and described them as *pre-seed* versus *Series A* funded, you probably form a mental image about the company along multiple dimensions. What's interesting is how different people can have fairly different mental images for the same funding phase. That's because there are wide variations in the uses of these descriptors, and they also change over time. Around the turn of the recent century, a Series A was raised well before a product was launched. Back then, the concept of a pre-seed funding round didn't even exist. Since I use these descriptors throughout the book, I need to provide my own parameters so that you know where I'm coming from. Just realize you will hear about and read different interpretations, which is only natural for the dynamic world of startups.

The best way to visualize a hypothetical startup's evolution is to start with the most pristine—but least likely—path from the idea phase through Series A funding. As you can see in figure 1.2, I'm using the metaphor of shifting gears through the evolutionary phases. The idea phase starts before raising money, while the next three phases each commence with a fundraising activity. The new funds provide the needed fuel (time and resources) to accomplish whatever will be needed to reach the sweet spot for the next round of funding. With each such boost of new fuel, the startup is able to shift a gear to move faster and do more things concurrently.

Figure 1.2. The early phases of startup fundraising

You'll notice that the shown sequence of funding stages ends with a Series A funding. Successful startups that want or need continued growth capital will later raise a Series B, Series C, and beyond, unless or until they no longer need external capital to fuel their growth or become sustainable.

IDEA

The idea stage doesn't usually start with, or require, external funding. Instead, it is the phase when your original idea gets formulated into an initial business plan and also when co-founders are sometimes recruited to the venture. It involves lots of customer discovery interviews and personal soul-searching to determine if the venture is worth pursuing in the first place. Bootstrapping is the most common method of funding this phase, and tons of startups never successfully exit this phase.

PRE-SEED

In the still-early days as you approach pre-seed funding, you have a developing idea but probably not even a working prototype. You need funding to build the prototype or a clunky, buggy, ugly, but minimally functional, minimum viable product (MVP) so that you can prove feasibility (can it be built?) and possibly start to get a sense for desirability (does anyone want it bad enough to pay for it?). During the idea phase, you should have completed enough customer discovery to refine the problem statement and to derive a huge list of assumptions as the starting business plan.

The pre-seed funding stage probably involves some planned continuation of bootstrapping (to reduce the amount of external funding needed) and the first outside funding, from friends and family and maybe some angel investors. You will be raising money mostly based on hope, vision, promise, and potential (let's call those HVPP for short). Investors will also highly evaluate you and your other team members' skills, experience, drive, and passion.

DEFINITION: ANGEL INVESTOR

Angel investors (often called simply *angels*) are high-net-worth individuals who allocate a portion of their personal net worth to investments in early-stage company ventures, such as startups. Many angels earn the moniker by also serving as an advisor to the startups they invest in.

Startups entering this phase don't have much in the way of operational maturity or method to their madness. It's possible they have an initial product development methodology and other very basic business processes, but since there isn't really any business yet, excessive processes and procedures just seem like unnecessary overhead.

Pre-seed funding rounds don't usually raise enough money to pay more than the smallest of salaries, which means most or all of the team members will still be working part-time on the venture.

Some pre-seed investors might require that at least one team member convert to full-time after the funding so as to demonstrate a real commitment.

A pre-seed funded startup spends most of its time getting the product into a form that's ready to launch but probably only has some basic form of product development methodology. Lining up the first beta customers is a key focus, and there should be time spent defining the initial strategy for acquiring customers and pricing the product.

SEED

To move from pre-seed to seed funding, you should have at least a working prototype product—your MVP. While working on your MVP, your product development methodology should have matured to the point of having a rhythm to your various product iterations. It is possible that you stretched your pre-seed stage long enough to actually get a v1 product launched into the market and with some first paying customers. If not, that will be a key theme for your seed round.

Seed investors will expect to see a fairly developed business plan and will closely evaluate the attributes of your team. The business plan should have matured to include important insights from your customer discovery, market size research, plans for customer acquisition, and one to two years' worth of financial projections. But you still have a lot of theories and assumptions that need to be validated. The investors can at least touch and feel your product and get a sense for how smart and driven your team is, but there is still some HVPP being evaluated.

A seed-funded startup usually has founders working full-time, but at way less than market-rate salaries, as well as some number of part-time employees and advisors that are equally passionate about the mission. New members get recruited to the team in order to fill various gaps and to allow the founders to each focus their energy on a smaller subset of the business. Everyone still wears multiple hats—just fewer of them. This slightly expanded team focuses a lot of attention on further proving desirability and starting to test for viability (is there a customer acquisition model that is sufficiently efficient and effective?).

It is common for the pricing strategy and general operational maturity to get refined during this phase as a result of repeated customer interactions throughout the sales cycle. You will start to get good at measuring and analyzing your unit economics for the customer acquisition-related functions. And hopefully you will start sending monthly updates to key stakeholders so they can better follow your progress. This includes both existing and potential future investors. It also means establishing and managing the business around a set of key performance indicators (KPI) for each function.

A startup should dramatically mature during the seed stage. Because of this, getting from the initial round of seed funding to the sweet spot for a Series A often takes long enough that a single round of funding is not sufficient. As a result, this total phase often involves multiple rounds of funding (i.e., seed 1, seed 2), each representative of a different set of accomplishments and operational maturity.

SERIES A

A Series A is usually the first equity round of funding for a startup and, therefore, often the first round that involves an institutional investor such as a venture fund. To catch their attention, you'll need a fairly complete operational dashboard with trended results for all KPIs. You should have regular strategy and planning meetings leading into a Series A, and you might even have practiced holding quarterly board of directors meetings, even if just with the founders and one or two advisors.

> **DEFINITION: EQUITY ROUND**
>
> An equity round is one in which an ownership interest (equity) in your company is sold to the investors. In order to calculate the amount of equity the investors will get, the company must first be valued (assigned a price tag). For this reason, we also refer to such rounds as a *priced round*.

Coming into a Series A, most key functions will be filled with full-time employees. The total team size might be as small as 10 or as large as 30, depending on the company's business model. A lot of Series A investors want to see $1–$2 million in annual revenue, because that is a level that demonstrates a repeatable and at least somewhat predictable customer acquisition process for most business models. Those targets can vary widely depending on the type of business (software versus hardware, B2B versus B2C, etc.), so only take it as a broad rule of thumb for stage-setting purposes.

A Series A-funded company continues significant focus on customer acquisition and revenue growth. I often use a spinning flywheel metaphor as the objective. You want to get a single flywheel spinning as efficiently as possible before seeking other expansion opportunities (more flywheels). Series A-funded companies often expand along some aspect of the business plan (product line, target customer, geographic market, etc.) to help accomplish the growth objectives. A first, truly strategic partnership often enters the picture and, if so, energy is applied so that it starts bearing fruit.

BEYOND SERIES A

Although the next phase is neither shown in figure 1.2 nor the focus of this book, you should assume that with each subsequent round of funding, the company reaches new revenue milestones and new levels of operational maturity. The specific priorities for any given Series B-funded (or later) startup vary greatly because of the wide variances of business models and associated company operations. Regardless, the purpose of subsequent funding rounds is continued growth and possibly a pursuit of profitability and sustainability. Beyond Series A, you'll have experienced executives on the team, and one will possibly take over as the new CEO.

MULTIPLE EVOLUTIONARY PATHS TO STARTUP GREATNESS

How many times have you read about a rocket ship company that's taking over the world? You get green with envy after imagining what it would be like to sit on that rocket ship and experience the near flawless execution that enabled their success. Fundraising was probably a breeze, and the best talent in the industry flocked to the company. What a utopian picture! But deep down, you know it virtually never works like that.

The evolutionary paths to startup greatness are something just shy of infinite and very rarely in a continuous, positive-sloped line. You'd be amazed to know how many supposed overnight successes were 10 years in the making—and with lots of twists and turns along the way. Your venture might have already encountered some twists and turns, and I want you to know that's totally normal and won't go away.

CHANGES OF DIRECTION

The best startups are adaptive, flexible, learning organisms. When they hit a dead end or some important assumption gets invalidated, they make an appropriate adjustment that's often called a *pivot*. While some pivots are actually just a minor tweak or fine-tuning, others are fundamental enough to the overall business plan that the company finds itself taking a few steps backwards before being able to step forward again.

In figure 1.3, you'll see that the pivot prevents making the planned gear shift and instead forces going around a metaphorical roundabout. This circular motion can continue multiple times before being ready to shift gears and move to the next phase. And if you're concluding that too many times around the roundabout without fresh funding could kill the company, you are correct. Even with fresh funding each time, you will feel the pain of additional dilution that otherwise wouldn't have been felt. But we do whatever it takes to stay alive and gain our most valuable resource, time.

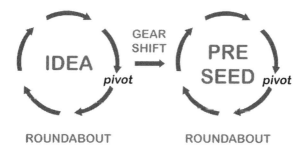

Figure 1.3. A pivot before a gear shift

BRIDGING PHASES

Sometimes (actually, oftentimes in the early days), we exhaust the available funds from the previous phase and discover that we haven't reached the sweet spot for the next phase. This means the next category or class of investors won't yet be excited enough to invest. But since we need extra time in order to reach that point, we need to raise additional funding. We typically call that a *bridge round*, and as you will see in figure 1.4, it is intended to bridge the identified gap. Such funding can be required even after the company is generating millions or even tens of millions in annual revenue.

Bridge rounds can also be very distracting and, because of that, the sooner you see the need coming, the better. This means you need to get good at forecasting revenue, expenses, product roadmap enhancements, new business partnerships, and the like.

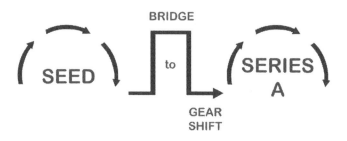

Figure 1.4. A bridge round

SKIPPING A GEAR

Have you ever skipped a gear while driving a car with a manual transmission? Doing so usually starts with achieving high enough RPMs while in one gear to be able to skip the next one. In other words, skipping straight from first to third gear, like figure 1.5 suggests.

What does this have to do with a startup venture? Well, like the metaphor suggests, there are times when a startup achieves so much acceleration and traction during a particular phase that they get to leapfrog over the next traditional round of funding. They still raise a round of funding but, like the figure suggests, a super-hot idea phase startup might be able to skip a pre-seed round of funding and go straight to a seed round. It's also possible that a hot pre-seed funded startup might be able to skip straight to a Series A.

These leapfrog opportunities are mostly only possible in the early phases of a company and not really something we talk about for companies that are generating millions of dollars. But just imagine the numerous benefits of being able to leapfrog: multiple interested lead investors and more favorable terms, more attractive to prospective employees, and less equity dilution, just to name a few. I bet you thought I was going to say it offers a faster path to $100 million in revenues. Yes, that too.

Figure 1.5. Skipping a stage

NUMEROUS SCENARIOS

At the outset of this section I suggested there are nearly infinite evolutionary paths for any given startup, and I expect now you see why. Multiple pivots and bridges are possible, including during the same phase. Hopefully either are later offset by a leapfrog, but those are very unusual—so don't count on one to save you.

To demonstrate how dramatically different the paths can be, below are two scenarios, one that we would all like to experience and another that is a little more typical.

Shockwave VR

1. Idea phase

2. Leapfrog to Seed phase

3. Gear shift to Series A phase

4. Gear shift to Series B phase

Shockwave AI

1. Idea phase

2. Pivot

3. Gear shift to Pre-Seed phase

4. Pivot

5. Bridge to Seed phase

6. Pivot

7. Bridge to Series A phase

8. Bridge to Series B phase

The differences are visually obvious, and you can imagine the extra time and funding it took Shockwave AI to approach their Series B phase. But, for fun, let's associate some assumptive metrics with each possible path through the evolution. We will use the following assumptions key:

- The idea phase lasts 3 months and carries a fundraising unit of 0.

- The pre-seed phase lasts 6 months and carries a fundraising unit of 1.

- The seed phase lasts 12 months and carries a fundraising unit of 3.

- The Series A phase lasts 24 months and carries a fundraising unit of 12.

- Each pivot lasts 50% of the time for that phase and carries a fundraising unit equal to 33% of the phase.

- Each bridge lasts 33% of the time for the prior phase and carries a fundraising unit equal to 33% of the phase.

If we apply the above assumptions to the two scenarios and round off the final numbers, here is the result:

- Shockwave VR: 39 months and 15 fundraising units

- Shockwave AI: 70 months and 23 fundraising units

I know this was just a hypothetical exercise, but I hope it helps you see the dramatic time and funding impact that repeated pivots and bridge rounds can have. One company got to a Series B in a little more than three years, while the other took almost six years and required 50% more funding to get there.

SUMMARIZING STARTUP SUCCESS

If anyone hands you a startup rulebook to follow or suggests there is a singular path to greatness, don't walk away. Run! This includes many things related to both fundraising and company operations. Even the ideas and best practices that I describe in this book are based on generalizations and my personal observations of several hundred startups over the past 19 years. One secret to your success will come from educating yourself on the fundamentals for best funding your venture while adjusting and adapting to your own situation.

Your evolution over time never, ever plays out as originally predicted. Your path will be more of a winding and bumpy road than a perfectly straight one. The less winding and bumpy, the better, but there will be curves, bends, hills, and gullies that weren't originally anticipated. As a result, flexibility and adaptability are superpowers that are either ideally exercised or must be quickly developed for basic survival and also future success.

If you decide to bootstrap your business venture during the very early days, great. It is nothing to be embarrassed about. In fact, this usually should be celebrated; it offers a lot of value to the founding team and early company culture. The entrepreneurs I admire most are consummate bootstrappers. The key is to determine when to evolve out of bootstrapping mode, assuming funding is needed to advance the business at the desired pace.

In the next couple of chapters, I will describe ways of planning for the various fundraising campaigns as your company evolves. Doing so will help keep your navigated path as straight and smooth as possible. That translates to needing less funding overall and more quickly reaching important evolutionary milestones along the way to building a great company.

AHA MOMENTS

1. There are countless ways of bootstrapping a venture, but receiving investment from friends and family is not one of them.

2. Equity dilution is almost always experienced as a result of issuing additional shares of stock into the company.

3. Validating the desirability and feasibility of your solution are the first required steps in the viability lifecycle of a new business.

4. The nomenclature used to describe the phase of a company or an associated stage of funding can vary. It has changed over time and will likely continue to do so.

5. Each stage of funding comes with a unique set of expectations related to team roles, operational maturity, and business results. Raising enough funding to reach the sweet spot for each subsequent stage is a key to fundraising success.

6. Business plan pivots and bridge funding rounds are tools to help a startup advance forward when things don't otherwise play out exactly as planned. Although they are common, they can be minimized via effective strategy and planning.

CHAPTER 2

FUNDRAISING STRATEGY

"A pessimist sees the difficulty in every opportunity;
an optimist sees the opportunity in every difficulty."

—Sir Winston Churchill

Y our first decision related to fundraising strategy is when to raise. This decision about timing is driven by one of two motivations: You either *need* to raise money or you *want* to raise money. Which is it in your case?

Most startups raise money because they need the funding to continue pursuing their dream. They require it either just to survive a while longer or to truly shift a gear and move into the next stage of evolution. If they don't raise funding, they will either have to abandon the mission or dial way back on their spending, which carries consequences of slower (even negative) growth and the risk of losing the market opportunity to competitors.

Some startups raise money even when they don't actually require it. Usually, this is because they either want to get more aggressive in their growth or because there's some opportunity they want to exploit sooner than when they might otherwise organically.

The need-versus-want decision first arises after the idea development stage, which is usually supported via bootstrapping. Some boot-strapped ventures discover they could continue in that mode longer, but the founders decide their situation is ripe for external funding in order to shift a gear into the pre-seed stage or possibly leapfrog to the seed stage. Other bootstrapped ventures have no choice but to raise funding either because the co-founders have exhausted their bootstrapping resources, the required amount of spending increases beyond the available bootstrapping resources, or one or more of the founders must jump into the venture full-time with some compensation in order for it to have a chance to progress.

After entering a particular stage, each subsequent stage is also preceded with the same *need versus want* situation. For a high-growth venture with the potential to get big, needing funding remains far more typical than wanting funding, at least through the Series B round and often beyond. Achieving both scalability and sustainability takes far longer and is far more difficult than most founders think.

Startups that choose to raise due to want rather than need have plenty of options. If they don't like the terms investors will agree to, they don't have to take on the additional capital. If the timing isn't right, they can delay. If they can't raise the amount desired, they can decide to raise less. But since most startups actually need to raise money, they don't have those options. They must be much more prescriptive in their fundraising strategy, or bad things can happen.

HOW MUCH SHOULD YOU RAISE?

Since deciding when to raise is usually clear, a much more difficult decision you will face is how much to raise. Not only is the decision critical to your own planning and forecasting, but investors will want to understand why you've chosen to raise the stated amount of money. Your ability to demonstrate that you determined the right amount of funding for the company at a particular stage is important for establishing credibility with the investor. You will essentially become the steward of their money through multiple rounds of funding, until you eventually exit and they get a return. They need to see a cohesive fundraising strategy that doesn't just let you survive for a while longer but rather allows you to reach future key milestones for continuing to get funded and eventually grow a great company. Investors get a lot of unacceptable responses when they ask why the desired amount of funding is the right amount, such as "most other startups at our stage seem to raise that amount," "it's the most we think we will be able to raise," "it only dilutes us 25%," or "it gives us one year of runway." These responses are possibly true, but they are all also terrible. I'm going to give you a framework for determining how much to raise and how to describe it to investors.

At this point in the process, you can operate somewhat in a utopian mindset. In other words, you will later get a chance to pitch investors for funding and might need to adjust your plans, but since you don't have their feedback at the beginning of the strategy process, you can start with more of a pristine, blank-page approach.

THE BASIC FORMULA

For startups seeking growth, figure 2.1 summarizes the first major steps for deciding how much to raise. As you can see, the amount of money you raise affords you a combination of time and resources. And with time and resources, you can accomplish things (outcomes).

Figure 2.1. How much to raise

The basic concept is simple. And since you're trying to solve for the right amount of funding to raise, let's analyze the other variables a little further.

TIME AND RESOURCES

When I say *time*, I actually mean an amount of time the money will last, or what is often referred to as *runway*. Every company's situation is different. But there are some typical amounts of runway associated with the various stages of fundraising. I only provide these so that you'll know if the investor is likely to think yours is longer or shorter than what they typically see. If so, it's not necessarily a problem as long as there is some sound logic that explains the difference.

- Pre-Seed: 6–9 months

- Seed: 12–18 months

- Series A: 18–24 months

- Series B: 24+ months

The most obvious type of resource is the one every founder obsesses about, additional headcount—regardless of whether they are part-time or full-time. "If we only had two more developers, we would be in great shape." In the same category as headcount are contractors, consultants, and various service professionals like lawyers and accountants. They contribute work and cost money but just aren't on the payroll as employees. What many early-stage startups don't think about are things like increased spending for marketing programs, specialty tools, and software systems. These are usually important resources that are also needed to advance the business.

Time and resources are in competition with each other. In other words, you could use all of the new funding to gain time, but that means not adding headcount to the team, not adding more contractors, and not spending more on programs, tools, and the like. Instead, you could use all of the new funding to aggressively dial up headcount and spending, but that means you'll almost immediately have to raise more money. So part of the trick is dialing in the optimal combination of extra time *and* extra resources in order to achieve the desired outcomes.

Figuring out the best combination involves creating a financial forecast model that allows you to experiment with various assumptions and alternatives. For a pre-seed or seed round of funding, you will have lots of assumptions that have no support from prior results. Because of this, the investors will really want to understand any information or insights you have to support your assumptions. Later, your prior track record will serve as a basis for many of your projections.

OUTCOMES

Outcomes are discretely identifiable results you hope to achieve with your newly raised funds. How about acquiring a certain number of new customers to reach the next meaningful revenue milestone or significantly reducing your average cost to acquire a new customer? How about securing a strategic partnership that will provide significant leverage or getting final approval on your patent filing? What about launching a new product or entering a new market? These are outcomes that reduce the investor's risk or increase their upside potential when you eventually exit.

The best way to understand the formula is the way it is diagramed above, left to right. But the best way to go about the exercise of figuring out how much money to raise is actually to work backwards, starting with the desired outcomes. It is those future outcomes that the investors want the company to achieve and, therefore, the things they want to fund. Once you've decided the future outcomes you want to reach with this round of funding, you simply need to use your financial forecast model to determine the best combination of time and resources needed to generate the outcomes. With this, determine how much funding you need for that combination of time and resources.

You will notice a dramatic difference in the outcomes that are expected by Silicon Valley investors versus most of the rest of the country. A set of future-expected outcomes that are exciting to an investor in Memphis, Tennessee, or Denver, Colorado, could easily seem way too safe and conservative to a Silicon Valley investor. This is because there is much more of a swing-for-the-fence, build a unicorn, and global world domination mentality in Silicon Valley. It is just a philosophical difference of risk-reward tolerance that should be understood by fundraising startups.

DON'T FALL INTO A TRAP

A common problem I see is startups that simply decide to raise enough money to last a specific amount of time, either with or without additional resources. So please don't just take my rule of thumb above for a seed round and dial in the amount of money that will last you 12 months. Investors care much less about how long your funding will last than what you're going to accomplish with it.

A factor to consider when deciding how much runway to gain is the fundraising activity itself. I'm talking about the next fundraising activity after your current one. If you wait to start your next round of funding until you've actually accomplished the outcomes, you'll be doing so with no cash in the bank. That doesn't work. And since it can easily take three to five months to raise a round of funding, you'll need to take this into consideration with your modeling. In other words, the right amount of funding basically needs to overshoot your desired outcomes by three to five months. Most startups ignore this important fact and end up having to raise money again in the future on less-than-ideal outcomes.

TIME FOR THE FIRST CHECK AND BALANCE

Why not just raise enough money to last a long time, like three or four years? Well, ignoring whether you could be successful raising that much, the answer relates to the valuation you're able to negotiate with investors.

DEFINITION: VALUATION

Your valuation is the implied value of your company. And since the value of your company is only what someone else is willing to agree it's worth, the valuation is most easily determined

continued

during fundraising events, an acquisition, or an IPO. During these activities, you and the investing parties must agree how much equity they will get for their investment. As a result, you will be effectively setting the value (valuation) of your company.

Let's assume $10 million would fund your venture for four years. The question is, What sort of valuation can you earn at the time you raise that money? As you can see in figure 2.2, today's valuation is mostly based on the state of your business today. If investors will only agree to a $5 million valuation, for example, you'll experience significant dilution and immediately give control of the company to the investors due to the amount of equity they will get. The amount of money you raise compared to the valuation you're able to negotiate provides a check and balance.

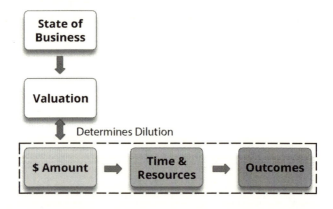

Figure 2.2. The influence of valuation

Because of this, the process of figuring out how much money to raise is often iterative. First, an uncontested look into the crystal ball allows you to figure out how much to raise in order to accomplish a desired set of outcomes. Next, a test-drive with investors helps inform whether the valuation you'll be able to negotiate derives reasonable dilution or if you'll need to adjust the amount, either up or down. If you adjust the amount down, the significance of the projected outcomes will also be adjusted down. That might cause the round of funding to seem less exciting for investors, and the iterations continue. The adjustments continue until you find the right balance of outcomes and valuation.

MULTIPLE ROUNDS OVER TIME

Now that you understand the basic formula and framework, let's project forward to see how multiple funding rounds tie together. As you can see in figure 2.3, with each round of funding, your projected outcomes eventually become the state of your business in the future. That is what you'll use to gain the desired step-up in valuation for the next round of funding. This cycle continues again and again until you are either self-sustaining or experience an exit (acquisition or IPO).

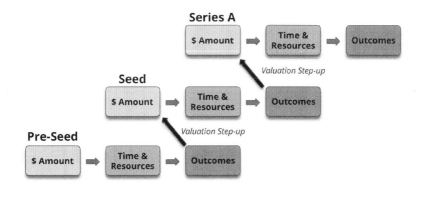

Figure 2.3. Multiple funding rounds over time

ELIMINATING SOME GUESSWORK

Even though you're operating somewhat in a utopian mindset at this point, I do recommend using a capitalization table simulator to run various scenarios. It will enable you to forecast what the cap table and various equity positions will look like after closing the next rounds of funding. It allows you to manipulate various assumptions for the amounts raised for multiple rounds of funding and the associated valuations. This removes the guesswork while also educating you on the various knobs and levers of fundraising and their effects on both founder and stakeholders' equity. It just helps takes the guesswork out of the process.

DEFINITION: CAPITALIZATION TABLE

More casually referred to as the *cap table*, this is a ledger that keeps track of the various equity holders in your company and their relative equity stakes (ownership percentages). This includes investors, advisors, and company employees alike—assuming all have some form of equity.

DON'T PUT THE FOCUS ON DILUTION

I find that a lot of fundraising founders get obsessively focused on dilution and make that the focal point for fundraising optimization. The problem with this approach is there are only two ways of optimizing for dilution. Either you push for a higher valuation, even if it's not quite deserved (subjective issue), or you decide to raise less money than originally planned. Pushing for an excessively high valuation will cause your fundraising efforts to take longer and potentially eliminate investor prospects that could serve you best (provide the most value). If instead you decide to raise less money, it will result in less runway or fewer and less significant outcomes—which will negatively affect you in the future.

As a result of what I've just described, I commonly preach the following mantra: Optimize for growth, not dilution. A great company with a track record of strong growth has infinite options. That's what you want and that's what your investors also want.

THE SCIENCE BEHIND THE ART

Fundraising strategy is as much art as science (probably more art in the very early stages). Realize that many of the concepts described here are part of fundraising science. Every situation is very different. However, based on the core principles described, below is a step-by-step sequence to consider for initially figuring out how much to raise for your next round of funding:

1. Decide which meaningful outcomes can and should be achieved next in order to position the company to raise money again at a considerably stepped-up valuation (double to triple the valuation for the current round).

2. Determine the combination of time and resources needed to accomplish those outcomes.

3. Put a price tag on step #2 to determine the amount of new funding needed.

4. Include an extra buffer amount of money to allow for surprises and the time to raise the next round of funding.

5. Sanity-check the proposed amount based on a reasonable range of valuations and the resulting dilution using a cap table simulator.

AVOIDING THE FUNDRAISING CHASM

Not much different from the famous chasm described in Geoffrey Moore's book *Crossing the Chasm*, funding your startup venture over time also presents a potential chasm to cross. This fundraising chasm doesn't trip up all startups, and just understanding that possibility is half of the battle during your fundraising strategy phase.

Investors tend to align their investment strategy with a specific round of funding. Some, but not many, cross over two rounds. And where there's crossover, it's not full crossover. In other words, Series A venture funds might invest in large seed rounds for companies that are well into the seed stage but not early seed-stage startups. Figure 2.4 below depicts the early funding stages and recaps some key attributes the investors typically evaluate for that stage.

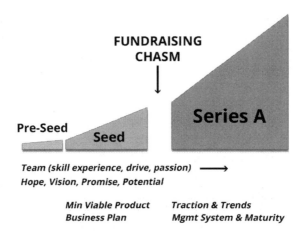

FUNDRAISING CHASM

Pre-Seed
Seed
Series A

Team (skill experience, drive, passion) ⟶
Hope, Vision, Promise, Potential

Min Viable Product　　　Traction & Trends
Business Plan　　　Mgmt System & Maturity

Figure 2.4. The fundraising chasm

There are several options for crossing the fundraising chasm, and they require either foresight or commonsense planning. You can adjust the target size of your seed-funding round, break it into multiple rounds, or bridge between rounds with a short-term funding solution.

OPTION 1: RAISE A LARGER SEED ROUND

If you want to go straight from a seed round to a Series A, the outcomes you plan to accomplish with the seed funding must be attractive to Series A investors. There are many outcomes that might seem impressive to you and might be far above where you are before raising your seed round. But if they're not what the Series A investors are looking for, you'll fall short and might end up in the chasm.

In fact, I think many companies actually have the right goals when they raise their seed round. But what often happens is things don't play out as expected. Product enhancement delays, market changes, team-related issues, distractions of a million varieties, and the like cause either a deviation of some sort (including a pivot) or a slowdown in progress. That means they don't accomplish the originally projected outcomes before they run out of money and, therefore, end up in the chasm.

DEFINITION: PIVOT

A pivot is a planned adjustment to some key aspect of the business plan. The magnitude of the pivot mirrors the magnitude or significance of the business plan adjustment. Pivots most often involve making adjustments for a new target market, customer acquisition strategy, or monetization strategy. But other adjustments to the business plan also can be considered pivots.

OPTION 2: PLAN FOR MULTIPLE SEED ROUNDS

It's possible that when you raise the initial seed round, you can predict that it won't be enough money to get you into a Series A sweet spot. Don't panic. In this case, from the beginning you can plan for multiple rounds of seed funding. I see this strategy quite regularly. With it, you can better avoid exceeding the sweet spot of most seed-stage investors but continue to earn some step-up in valuation based on your accomplishments. You will want to make it clear to the first round of seed investors that this is your strategy, because they are your most likely candidates for the second seed round.

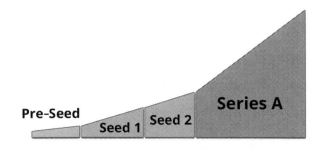

Figure 2.5. Multiple seed rounds

OPTION 3: BRIDGE THE GAP WITH A SMALL SEED ROUND

This is a reactive strategy rather than a proactive one. There's a reason a certain form of funding is referred to as a *bridge round*. It is intended to bridge the gap between where you are and the next most logical/desirable time to raise money. It usually funds a shorter amount of time than is suggested for a second seed round—in this case, raising enough money to safely cross the fundraising chasm and be better positioned for a Series A. Don't set a strategy based on raising a future bridge round, because they aren't as easy to accomplish as it might seem. Just know that it's a tool in your toolkit, if needed.

Hopefully you've concluded that the fundraising chasm is at least something to take into consideration during your seed fundraising strategy. Things won't play out like you plan, and that's why "raise more than you think you'll need" is common advice given to founders during the early stages. And the people who say that are probably doing so because they got trapped in the fundraising chasm at some point in their past. It's true that you will be diluted more by raising more than you think you need, and it's also possible the interest from investors isn't sufficient to raise more than you think you'll need. But at least spend some time thinking this through so as to minimize the odds of dealing with the chasm later.

SUMMARIZING STARTUP SUCCESS

Evolving from a bootstrapped startup to a funded one is a big and important transition. You might end up as a funded startup out of need or want. If you don't need funding, then you have alternatives. Most startups eventually need outside funding and, once that happens, many things change. One of those things is you get to accomplish more and grow faster, assuming you have a scalable business. But you will also experience a change in accountability. No longer are you only accountable to yourself and your other team members; now you have to answer to your new investors, who might have different interests, beliefs, and motivations than you. The more investors you take on over time, the more varied those interests, beliefs, and motivations will be, and the more you'll have to accommodate or negotiate with them.

There is a lot that can go into your fundraising strategy phase. But, like many things in business, up-front time and effort spent on strategy can pay huge dividends later. This translates to increased odds of raising the right amount of money to reach the next significant milestone for making another want-versus-need decision and generally controlling your destiny. Surely you know things won't play out exactly as planned, but that doesn't relieve you from the obligation to start with a strategy. After that, you can do what every great entrepreneur does—adjust and adapt as necessary.

I mentioned likely iterations to your strategy that are due to test-driving some ideas and assumptions with investors before actually launching the fundraising campaign. That takes place during the planning phase of your campaign and is what we will cover in the next chapter.

 ## AHA MOMENTS

1. The amount you raise affords a combination of time (runway) and resources (people, programs). With time and resources, you can achieve future outcomes.

2. Investors write checks for outcomes, not activities.

3. In order to figure out the right amount to raise, work the model backwards by starting with a desired set of outcomes. Then determine the optimal combination of time and resources needed to achieve them. Then put a price tag on the plan.

4. Expectations related to outcomes and the associated risk-reward vary greatly depending on location, with Silicon Valley investors being the most aggressive.

5. Your future fundraising activity will take time, which means you must take that into account when deciding how much to raise in the near-term round. Otherwise, you will start raising your future round before having accomplished the desired outcomes.

6. The list of desired outcomes must be sufficient to reach the next logical funding stage and at a considerably stepped-up valuation. Falling short might put you in the fundraising chasm.

7. The sweet spot gap between the seed and Series A stages is so vast that many startups proactively plan two or more seed rounds of funding.

8. Too much focus on dilution can obscure your long-range mission of building a great company. Optimize for growth, not dilution.

9. Due to the significant unpredictability with early-stage ventures, it is almost always best to raise more than you think is necessary, assuming the investor demand is there.

CHAPTER 3

PLANNING YOUR CAMPAIGN

"No battle was ever won according to plan,
but no battle was ever won without one."

—General Dwight Eisenhower

A successful fundraising campaign at any stage of funding has a rhythm. It has a start, a middle, and an end. It is critical to understand and plan that rhythm along with the associated time commitment before launching the campaign. Entrepreneurs are taught to move fast and break things, but doing so with your fundraising campaign will actually deliver on the stated promise: It will break things.

Instead, take your time and plan for the actual activities that will comprise your campaign. One of the most important activities is finding the right investors for your upcoming stage. Engaging investors that aren't good prospects is a waste of time, and time is both the most valuable resource a startup has and one that usually isn't plentiful.

ALLOCATING TIME AND PRIORITY

Maintaining the proper rhythm throughout your fundraising campaign involves careful allocation of both time and priority. Like any good entrepreneur, you know things won't play out exactly according to the plan, but having a plan helps you figure out when it's time to adapt on the fly.

BEFORE YOU BEGIN: PICK A TEAM CAPTAIN

During the pre-seed and seed stages of funding, it might be obvious who will lead the fundraising efforts for your startup, but that might be because there is only one full-time member of the team. If, instead, there are multiple co-founders but no one individual carries the CEO title (versus just "founder"), only one person should bear the burden of being the fundraising *lead*. Trying to share the duty will be as ineffective as rotating sales reps each week for a million-dollar opportunity with a large enterprise, or rotating football quarterbacks with each play. You've got to get into a rhythm, which means context switching isn't helpful.

This doesn't mean investors won't want to meet and interact with other members of the team; they will. But the chief fundraiser leads the process and is the frontline person for most interactions. They will develop relationships with prospective investors in the early phase of fundraising, and the best of those relationships will carry forward to closed investments.

Once a founder adopts the title of CEO, she will become the chief fundraiser by default. Being the CEO and serving as the chief fundraiser go hand in hand throughout the life of the company. Investors want to evaluate and get to know the CEO more than any other member of the team. That doesn't mean the other founders and executives aren't important to the investors. It just means the CEO is under greater scrutiny than the others and is, therefore, the one the investors most want to interact with during their evaluation. So if you're an introverted and amiable founder who doesn't like controversy, doesn't have at least some charisma, and has trouble coping with repeated rejection, you will need another founder to be the chief fundraiser. This probably means they should also adopt the CEO title.

START: DETERMINE INVESTOR INTEREST

The purpose of the first phase is relationship building, and it should consume about 20% of your time. Over the course of a month or two, you should try to determine which investors could be viable prospects, and you accomplish this by meeting with them before you're actually ready to hit them up for investment. In fact, you should make that clear when you reach out to them by saying something like "We're not raising money at the moment, but I wanted to see if I could spend some time with you to let you know what we're working on and to get your feedback."

With the understanding that you're not going to ask them to write a check at the end of the meeting, investors will give you some of the most honest feedback possible. Their questions, concerns, level of excitement, body language, and—hopefully—a twinkle in their eye will inform you as to their level of interest. Organize all of this information across lots (possibly dozens) of meetings so that you're ready for the next phase.

Even when you're not executing a fundraising campaign, you should always operate in some level of relationship building. You don't need to spend a full 20% of your time meeting prospective investors for a round of funding that is a year or more away, but you should always be seeking and building relationships for just that reason. You're likely going to need to raise money again in the future. The most successful startups I work with are perpetually fundraising, which means that, even when they aren't actively executing a campaign, they're building and grooming their investor pipeline for the next round.

MIDDLE: PREPARATION AND PRIORITIZATION

The purpose of this phase is to take your campaign on a test-drive while setting the environment for the final phase in which you'll actually hit up investors for money. Over the course of some number of weeks, you should interact with the most interested investors from the first phase to get the next level of needed feedback. If you're raising a small round and have fewer than 10 interested investors, it might only take a couple of weeks. For a larger round that includes interested institutional investors, it could take a month or more.

This phase should consume 30%–40% of your time. And if you are fundraising out of need instead of want, your level of stress will increase because, by now, you're definitely watching your cash fume date and the stakes are getting higher.

DEFINITION: CASH FUME DATE

This is the date you project to run out of money. There are two ways to calculate the cash fume date. One assumes that you acquire no new customers in the future; the other assumes that you achieve your forecasted sales targets. Many companies calculate both in order to understand the variance in runway allowed.

Your interactions with investors will be more specific as a result of exposing them to the amount of money you decided to raise, your key proposed terms, and the milestones you expect to reach with new funds. In some cases, you will communicate ranges, so as to not lock yourself in and to still allow investor feedback. Examples include the amount you plan to raise and your proposed valuation. You will also set expectations for when you plan to officially launch the fundraising campaign and need to get more specific in gauging the investors' interest. Done correctly, by the end of this phase you will have a prioritized list of investors (by likelihood to invest), a specific amount to raise, and a final set of proposed terms.

END: ASK FOR MONEY

Too many startups begin their campaign by pitching to investors and hitting them up for investment while adjusting and adapting their proposed terms along the way. Not only is this inefficient, but it burns bridges with too many investors. It's not very effective to come back to an investor after a failed pitch to inform them that you changed your mind about the terms and now they're more attractive. It's best to measure twice and cut once for something as important as a fundraising campaign.

This phase should consume *at least* 80% of the chief fundraiser's time. That means your co-founders and other team members have to pick up your workload. Let me be really clear on this. You cannot dial in this phase of fundraising at only 50% of your time. If you execute the prior phases effectively and if you've got a sound investment opportunity, you should have created momentum that you must capitalize on aggressively. I know that means your business won't advance at the same pace as before, and this is another reason to get aggressive on closing your funding round. Run on the hamster wheel as fast as possible until you either close the round or there's no more interest from high-odds investors.

This phase has the most variability in the length of time required. I've seen seed and Series A rounds close in 30 days, and I've seen them take six months—and that's after first completing the start and middle phases of your fundraising journey.

IT TAKES MUCH LONGER THAN YOU THINK

Although I mentioned seeing some funding rounds close in 30 days *after* the preparation phase, those are definitely the exception. If you add up the time allotment for all three phases of fundraising, you should expect it to take at least four months and probably more like six. You should also prepare for the possibility of losing momentum at 50%–75% of your funding goal and needing an additional two to three months to fully close the round. It almost always takes much longer than founders think to close a round of funding.

IDENTIFYING PROSPECTIVE INVESTORS

Much like a marketing campaign that has an objective of securing new customers, your fundraising campaign could be graphically diagramed as a funnel. You've got to start by filling the top of the funnel with prospective investors. If you can't find them, you can't build a relationship with them. And just like a marketing campaign, the quality of the prospects makes a big difference to the efficiency and effectiveness of the campaign. Optimizing the mix of quantity and quality of investor prospects is going to take a lot of research and a lot of hustle. Hopefully this isn't a surprise.

YOUR IDEAL TARGETS

Most investors are stage-specific. In other words, they only invest in seed-stage companies or only in Series A companies. So let's start by listing the most common types of investors by funding stage.

PRE-SEED

Friends and family are the most likely source of investment during this phase. However, don't take investments from just anyone willing to support you; in many cases, they must be accredited investors as defined by the US Securities and Exchange Commission (SEC). Crowdfunding portals can be a good solution for some startups that haven't launched their product, but you'll need to do your research to compare the options and to make sure your product is a good candidate for presales via crowdfunding. Government grants are also a possibility, and you'll need to do research to find the right programs. Angel investors are a possibility, but you will learn shortly that only a very small subset of angels will participate in a pre-seed round—and they aren't easy to find.

I have to give a warning and strong recommendation here: If you decide to seek friends and family for part or all of your pre-seed funding, please tell them three times to their face that, at this very early phase, the odds are high that you won't be able to pay them back. If they still definitely want to support you by investing, go for it. Without the repeated warnings, future family holiday dinners and college sorority reunions can become really uncomfortable if you are not one of the startups that beat the death odds. Also make sure to involve your attorney regarding possible accredited investor issues and proper investment instruments to use. Lots of pre-seed funding rounds end up with issues that must get fixed later.

DEFINITION: ACCREDITED INVESTOR

At the time of this writing, for most investments into private companies in which equity is being sold, the US securities laws stress the importance of doing so only with investors that are "accredited." There are various financial tests to determine investor qualification, and the spirit of the laws is to protect those who don't have enough net worth to be investing in one of the riskiest asset classes, like startup venture investing. Search the SEC website for the current qualification criteria and consult with your attorney to make sure you don't accidentally jeopardize your company's future by taking investment from the wrong people or using the wrong process.

SEED

Angel investors are the dominant source of investment for the seed stage. They can invest solo or as part of an angel network or syndicate. Angels that are investing solo usually only do so in their areas of expertise, which usually means startup ventures that somehow overlap with their own professional career. Their online biography or LinkedIn profile can serve as a good source of information for filtering and rating them. Startup accelerators can also be a viable source of a portion of your seed funding because acceptance into the program is often accompanied with an investment. Many accelerators focus on a particular industry or technology, which brings additional value versus just their investment. Finally, there are some venture funds and family offices that invest in seed-stage startups, although they are in the minority.

DEFINITION: FAMILY OFFICE

A family office is a wealth management and investing function for ultra-high-net-worth individuals (think billionaires or close). They are managed by an investment professional, a staff of professionals, or an outsourced firm. From the perspective of a startup, they operate similarly to a venture fund but with their funding from a high-net-worth individual rather than a collection of investors that are called *limited partners*.

SERIES A

Venture funds are the dominant source of investment for Series A funding. They usually have one or more areas of focus with their investment strategy. This can be along industry lines (healthcare, education, real estate), technologies (artificial intelligence, virtual reality, robotics), business models (ecommerce, marketplaces, tech licensing), solution types (mobile apps, SaaS, hardware), customer segments (consumer, small- to medium-size businesses [SMB], enterprise, government), or just about any aspect of a business plan you can think of. The good news is that venture funds make it easy to decode their investment strategy just by reading their website and looking at their existing portfolio of investments.

Regardless of the funding stage you're in, your mission is to find the *right* investors to meet with rather than just anyone that invests in startups. It's just like targeting customers to buy your solution. You should be laser focused rather than broad. Do your research with each prospect you identify, and prioritize them according to how aligned their investment strategy is with your business. Your most valuable resource is actually time (runway). That's because with enough time, you can adjust, adapt, and eventually figure out a path to viability. Don't waste your valuable time on low-odds investors.

WHERE DO YOU FIND THEM?

Venture funds, angel networks, crowdfunding portals, and government grant programs are all searchable online. Your success finding the best targets is mostly a matter of effort. It is the individual angel investors that are much more difficult to find, at least the best ones for a specific startup. That's because they don't have websites and openly published investment criteria. In fact, they aren't always actively investing, so even if you find a perfect match, she might not be investing at the time you need the money.

To find the best angels, you have to go where they hang out. Some are members of angel networks or similar angel investing syndicates. And even though they sometimes invest with a group, many of them invest individually as well. Some are affiliated with startup incubators and accelerator programs, probably as a mentor or maybe in a leadership role. Some serve as a judge for pitching events and hackathons. If you get involved with those same groups and activities, you will meet angel investors.

If the city you live in doesn't have many of these activities or events, it's going to be a lot more difficult. Angel investors very much like to invest locally so they can keep tabs on their investments while actively helping their portfolio of startups as an advisor of sorts. This means angels from elsewhere in your state or a neighboring state might still be candidates, but your challenge is going to be more difficult.

NETWORK, NETWORK, NETWORK

Did I mention that it's important to network? Networking is critical to fundraising success at all stages other than a pre-seed round that's funded by friends and family who already know you. So if you are introverted, now is the time to either get used to being uncomfortable or find a co-founder who can lead the fundraising efforts. Attending pitching events and hackathons as a spectator but not mixing and mingling as much as possible isn't going to help you find your investors. The same thing holds for going to social events hosted by angel networks and only talking to one or two of the participating angels.

Networking is also the best way to get access to your ideal venture funds. Introductions from people in their own network bring far greater odds of getting a meeting than an unsolicited email. This means you first have to impress the people in their network so that they will be willing to make the introduction. You've got to put yourself out there, even if it's not in your nature. The success of your company depends on it!

PRE-SEED INVESTORS ARE ESPECIALLY HARD TO FIND

Raising money from professional investors before your product is built, launched, and generating revenue is far more difficult than when those things have already been accomplished. This can result in dozens or even hundreds of investor pitches that do not meet with success. The pre-seed stage is often the hardest phase for raising external capital, and this is the reason many startups decide to either continue bootstrapping through the whole phase or find alternate sources of funding, such as a presales campaign or a government grant.

THE CHALLENGES

Early-stage investors understand the high-risk nature associated with their investments, so that's not the big issue. But they are also looking for the right trade-off between risk and reward. Below are some things an investor might seek in order to optimize both risk and reward:

- Optimizing (reducing) risk: They might look for an experienced full-time team with a successful track record or for paying customers of the product.

- Optimizing (increasing) reward: They might look for a huge market size or a valuation lower than normal.

The problem is that during the pre-seed stage, the best you could do is approximate the list above, and that's assuming you can assemble a full-time team that's working only for equity. You could have a huge market and a low valuation, but you won't yet have paying customers from a launched product. If this hypothetical investor sticks to the optimized risk-reward criteria, they will seek startups at the seed stage, not the pre-seed stage. For this reason, you need a special type of angel investor.

INTRODUCING THE
"HYPER-INTERSECTED" ANGEL

The term *hyper-intersected* doesn't exist in the dictionary. It is a term I often use when describing the type of angel investor that has the highest propensity to consider a pre-seed-stage investment. It is basically an investor that is able to uniquely lower their risk factor due to having some close affinity (intersection) with one or more attributes of your business plan. This changes their own risk-reward equation in a way that allows them to consider a pre-seed investment rather than wait until the attributes of a traditional seed-stage investment are met.

I'll give you a personal example. I spent most of my professional career selling enterprise hardware and software solutions to Fortune 1000 organizations using either a direct sales or channel distribution method of acquiring customers. I am more comfortable and capable of interrogating pre-seed-stage startups that have those attributes in their business plan. As a result, I also feel like I'm better at assessing their possibility of building a viable, scalable, and sustainable business—one that could eventually exit and make everyone a lot of money. I would not feel as comfortable or capable with a pre-seed-stage startup that's building a mobile app for consumers, because I've never been in that movie before as an operator.

OPPORTUNITIES FOR "INTERSECTION"

You're looking for angel investors who are knowledgeable about as many aspects of your venture as possible and who can bring their connections along with them. For example, the investor could know *you* really well; friends and family are obviously the best example, but possibly so are current or prior close business associates. They already know your style, personality, and what makes you tick, so you don't have to convince them that you're smart, ethical, willing to work hard, and super passionate about the problem you're solving. Pre-seed investors that don't already know you really well will need to intersect (have a close affinity) with one or more elements of your business plan.

INDUSTRY

I'm talking about the industry vertical you will sell into, such as education, healthcare, or financial services. Investors that have spent time in your industry understand the subtle nuances of how the industry works, who the major players are, how money is made, and the like. If you also know the industry, you and the investor will speak the same language, and they'll be able to really dive deep with you on your strategy and plan of attack. Better yet, they'll know that if they decide to invest, they can help introduce you to their network and generally help you in various other ways as an informal advisor.

TARGET CUSTOMER

If you're building a horizontal solution (not uniquely focused on specific industries), seek angels that know the type of customer you will target: corporations, government institutions, SMB, or consumers. Your strategies for customer acquisition and support become important in this regard. They must be aligned with your target customer. For example, many solutions sold to consumers use self-service customer acquisition methods, whereas expensive solutions sold to the government require public procurement processes. Investors that understand the type of customer you are targeting will best be able to evaluate your plans for implementing processes and tools related to customer acquisition and support.

PRODUCT CATEGORY

Each different product category is accompanied by a unique product development process and pricing strategy that the angel will understand well. Examples include consumer electronics, mobile apps, data center hardware, CPG, medical devices, enterprise SaaS software, and professional services.

BUSINESS MODEL

Similar to target customers, business models are driven by unique customer acquisition methods and monetization strategies. Examples of business models include two-sided marketplaces, technology licensing, direct sales, self-service, and retail distribution. If you're building a technology-licensing business, for example, investors that have done the same will understand the nuances of licensing and pricing models, exclusivity requests, and joint-development processes. If, instead, you will sell your product through retail distribution, investors that have done the same will understand the importance of just-in-time inventory, endcap displays, and consumer incentive strategies.

TECHNOLOGY

Technology is different from product category. Examples of technology include artificial intelligence (AI), virtual reality (VR), and blockchain. If your solution heavily leverages technologies like these, investors who also understand them will appreciate the unique value they can bring to your customers and what your roadmap of product enhancements might entail. They will also know the big industry players who could later serve as value-add partners.

IMPROVING YOUR ODDS

Imagine if you found an angel investor that matched more than half of the above criteria. Your odds of getting them to invest are infinitely higher than an investor who doesn't match any of the criteria. The odds of a pre-seed investor getting serious about making an investment are directly proportional to the number of checkmarks you can place next to the criteria listed above. You are basically trying to thread a needle with a piece of rope; it's easier if you tease it apart. That's one of the reasons why pre-seed rounds are so difficult.

There are a few situations that even intersected pre-seed investors will regard as riskier than normal. If any of these situations apply to you, you're going to need even more instances of intersection. If you just got started and are barely past the blank sheet of paper and don't yet have any real semblance of a business plan, team, customer interview feedback, or product requirements, investors will assess a much higher risk, because all you really have is hope and the founders' personal track records of success.

If your solution will serve a niche market, your market size will be smaller than the investor desires, and they'll worry about future market expansion opportunities. On the other hand, if the product you are building solves a problem the world doesn't really recognize exists, the investor will worry about the extra time, energy, and capital you'll need to put into grassroots evangelism to help generate the needed awareness.

If you expect a long time before launching your product, investors will be concerned with the extra amount of money you'll need to raise over multiple rounds of funding to reach that point. Failure during any one of those funding rounds kills the company. Examples of such companies are those building complex hardware products or healthcare solutions that require FDA approval. Products like this can take years before they are ready to launch. These issues are not complete disqualifiers, but rather narrow the field of possible pre-seed investors even further. This is because the more issues you need to overcome, the greater the level of hyper-intersection is required.

As you can probably imagine, finding hyper-intersected angels is not easy. It's unbelievably difficult, because the more criteria you need to match, the fewer candidates there are—and angel investors don't walk around with a sign around their neck informing you about the ways they might intersect with you. You're going to need to be driven, creative, scrappy, and unstoppable if you're going to have a chance of applying the principles suggested here. The good news is those are the same attributes you need to build a successful business anyway.

SUMMARIZING STARTUP SUCCESS

Like with the strategy phase, time spent planning out the actual fundraising campaign will pay dividends by improving your odds of success at raising the desired amount from the right investors and in an efficient manner. Successful campaigns have a certain rhythm, which must be planned ahead of time. Refer to figure 3.1 for my typical recommendation. The time allocation and level of effort exerted during the start, middle, and end phases are analogous to a sport race. I am a long-time competitive swimmer, and when I compete in a middle- or long-distance race, I carefully plan out my desired pace during the start, middle, and end of the race. It is my effort and exertion during the race that dictates the pace. Executed perfectly, I touch the wall with both a best time and a gold medal.

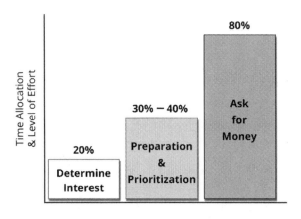

Figure 3.1. Campaign phases

Don't randomly start pitching investors before you're prepared, and don't pitch investors until you've planned out your campaign. If you do so, you risk losing credibility and wasting time. Credibility with prospective investors is absolutely required, and time is your most valuable resource; a lack of planning is a double whammy. I would rather see you tell a prospective investor you haven't yet launched your round of funding but would love to get to know them better rather than have you try to formally pitch them unprepared just because they expressed some interest.

Your mission isn't just to find any investor that has a heartbeat and breathes, but rather the right investors that have reasonable or better odds of investing. Time wasted on low-odds investors is a killer. The described phases of a successful campaign are intended to help identify the best investors in the most efficient manner. This is especially difficult during the pre-seed stage, when you don't have any real validation of viability.

A fundraising campaign almost always involves a lot more time and effort than anticipated. Mentally prepare yourself for a grind through lots of meetings and lots of rejection. But know that each positive meeting you have results in a bit of a battery recharge, and that, combined with the fire you already have in your belly, will propel you through the fundraising grind.

 AHΛ MOMENTS

1. Only one person should serve as the chief fundraiser. If the company has someone with a CEO title, it's them.

2. Not all startup CEOs have the required core strengths needed to successfully fundraise. Time for soul-searching.

3. Successful fundraising campaigns have a start, middle, and end phase.

   a. The start is focused on determining interest and consumes about 20% of the chief fundraiser's time.

   b. The middle consumes 30%–40% of time and is focused on rating prospective investors and gaining feedback on both the amount to be raised and the key terms.

   c. The end requires dialing up to 80% in order to close out actual investments.

4. Fundraising campaigns operate like a marketing or sales funnel, with a mix of investor quantity and quality.

5. Your most valuable resource is time. With enough time, you can adjust and adapt until you generally identify a viable, scalable, and sustainable business model.

6. In order to find investors, you have to go where they hang out.

7. Prepare to network, network, network until you're sick of it. Then network a little more.

8. If you can't bootstrap all the way through the pre-seed phase, seek hyper-intersected angel investors. Their odds of investing are directly proportional to the amount of affinity (intersection) they have with various elements of your business plan.

CHAPTER 4

YOUR FUNDRAISING TOOLKIT

"Luck is what happens when preparation meets opportunity."

—Seneca, first-century Roman philosopher

N o carpenter goes to a home-building site without a tool belt full of construction tools. No painter walks to the canvas without a cadre of brushes and paints. No comedian steps onstage without a rehearsed set of jokes. Fundraising is no different: You need a belt full of tools, a palette full of colorful stories, and maybe even a joke or two.

Your most important fundraising tools will be your elevator pitch, pitch deck, and financial projection model. If crafted and used correctly, your toolkit will not only serve as a helpful guide but also become a difference maker in your fundraising efforts by setting you apart from others that don't put in the same effort.

YOUR ELEVATOR PITCH

There's a reason it's referred to as an *elevator pitch*; it's meant to be a succinct description of your venture that can be delivered on a short elevator ride with a potential investor. Your elevator pitch must be expressed in a few sentences so that it takes no more than 15 to 20 seconds to deliver. And that might even be a little generous. Psychologist Michael Formica reported that the average non-task-oriented attention span of a human being is about 8 seconds. You might hear about a 90-second elevator pitch. To me, that's just a short version of your full pitch but not really an *elevator* pitch.

I have a mantra about effective elevator pitches. They only need to accomplish one thing: They need to generate enough interest with the recipient to cause them to ask you a question—any question. With that, you might get an additional two to three minutes to expand further and hopefully generate enough additional interest for a full-blown conversation. It doesn't matter if that extended conversation happens right away or at a later time.

Let's say you and I get on an elevator on the ground floor, and we're both going to the sixteenth floor. You happen to recognize me and say something like "Hey, are you Gordon Daugherty, author of that book on startup fundraising?"

"As a matter of fact, I am," I'd respond. "Who are you?"

"I'm Meagan," you might say (if your name is Meagan), "founder of Shockwave VR."

As I respond with "Cool, what does Shockwave VR do?," the elevator doors close and your eight-second clock starts ticking.

When we get to the sixteenth floor and the elevator doors open, one of two things happens. I either say something like "Nice to meet you, Meagan. Good luck with your startup venture," and walk to the break room for coffee, or I take a side step after exiting the elevator and say something like "That sounds interesting. How do you X?" It doesn't matter what X is. You've triggered enough interest that I've asked a question. That's your opening for a more expansive pitch.

Did you notice how binary the outcome is? I either walk away—potentially forever—or I give you a chance to tell me more and, therefore, hopefully get me excited enough to exchange business cards and suggest that we get together for coffee to continue the discussion.

TWO SENTENCES WILL DO IT

A lot of startup founders overthink their elevator pitch. They feel like it must close the deal by incorporating anything and everything of possible interest for a variety of audiences. The opposite is true. Too much information actually makes it less interesting for some audiences and causes it to surpass a normal human's attention span. Coming up with something short and compelling is actually much harder than something more broad and complete. It reminds me of Mark Twain's quote: "I apologize for such a long letter—I didn't have time to write a short one."

Remember, you only have 8 to 10 seconds of attention, and you only need to generate enough interest to raise a question. I recommend that you come up with two sentences that answer the following questions:

WHAT DO YOU DO?

My Capital Factory colleague, Mikey Trafton, teaches startups to simplify their approach to this sentence using the following format: "We help (customers) solve (problem) for (benefit)." An alternative format I sometimes use is "We created (a product) for (target customers) so they can gain (result)."

Easy, right? Just fill in the placeholders with your info. Actually, it is much harder than most people think, because they are burdened by all of the knowledge they possess. Simplifying a complex project you've spent the last year (or more) on into a couple of phrases requires that you focus on your audience. It doesn't matter which part of the venture is most intriguing to *you*; which part of it would be interesting to an outsider? What do they most need to know to understand the problem you are solving?

SO WHAT?

Beyond the simple purpose of your venture, you have to describe why it's important. Why should someone care about what you're doing? The answer might be a little different depending on whether you're talking to a prospective customer, a business partner, or an investor. But it must complement your first sentence that describes what you do, and it should be compelling enough to give the other person no choice but to ask a question. Try making a bold claim or bragging about some results you've achieved.

Here is an example: Shockwave Innovations helps educate, advise, and fund tech startups so they can maximize their odds of success. One startup we helped during their founding days reached $65 million in revenue and a NASDAQ IPO.

It's actually a true story, and what I'm hoping for is a response like "Wow, which company is it?" or "What was their IPO valuation?" or "NASDAQ or New York Stock Exchange?" or "How are they doing now?" It totally doesn't matter what question they ask because it gains two to three minutes of additional, valuable time with which to engage the investor.

Here's another example, this one completely made up: DoggieDrone enables dog owners to take their dog on a walk around the neighborhood without ever leaving the house. You get to select the distance, speed, and route, then let the drone do the rest while you watch on your mobile device.

Hopefully, you're already thinking of two or three questions you're dying to ask.

To help identify the most compelling options for your elevator pitch, try using my "so what?" test. After reciting the elevator pitch to yourself, imagine that someone responds, "So what? Why should I care?" Your answer to this question might belong in the elevator pitch. I regularly hear elevator pitches that have too much "what" and not enough "so what." Make sure they understand not just *what* you do but *why*.

KEEP IT SIMPLE AND CONVERSATIONAL

Don't use complicated industry or technical jargon; keep your vocabulary around an eighth-grade level. You want to pique their interest, not glaze their eyes. Even if your potential investor is an industry professional, you should be able to discuss your venture in clear, simple language. Otherwise, it may seem that you are focused on the mechanics of the problem rather than a meaningful fix. Think like a layman, not an expert.

You can write down your elevator pitch, but remember that how we write is often different from how we speak. Simplified language goes a long way toward making a short prepared speech feel like a spontaneous conversation. You want your elevator pitch to sound natural, in the conversation sense. And like any business conversation, what you say should be clear, convincing, and relevant to the specific person you're talking to.

You should also try to be specific and targeted rather than casting a wide net. To take that fishing analogy further, a net is meant to scoop up everything in its path. But with an elevator pitch, you're trying to hook just one special fish, which requires a single hook and the right bait for that specific fish. If your net is too wide, they're likely to wriggle through the holes. For example, if you sell multiple products to multiple types of customers, pick the single most important product and customer type for your elevator pitch. After you get a question, you'll have a chance to inform about the other aspects of your business.

You can also try to quantify your claims with numbers or factoids. They help certain claims sink in better and often help facilitate the desired question. But remember to keep it simple: Don't just list a bunch of figures. Focus on one or two crucial and impressive numbers.

TIME FOR A TEST-DRIVE

After working in an isolated environment, it's time to take your elevator pitch on a test-drive so that it can be refined. Here is an experiment to try. Recite your elevator pitch to 20 people who don't have much prior knowledge about your idea or your company. They don't have to be complete strangers. Maybe do this with your neighbors, relatives, former coworkers, and so on. Ask them to react with the first question that comes to mind, but don't answer their question right away. Instead, next ask them to tell you what they think your company does from only hearing the elevator pitch. Are you getting the questions you want? Are they in the right ballpark with regard to their guess about what you do? If not, make changes to your elevator pitch until you're satisfied.

You might get lots of similar questions from your experimental subjects. That's good; it means that your pitch is triggering the same ideas with multiple people. But more importantly, are they the right questions? Do they allow you to elaborate on the crucial parts of your venture? If not, you may need to adjust the pitch to elicit better questions.

You can then work on answering the questions in a way that keeps the conversation moving forward. Try out a few different ways of phrasing the answer to a common question. Does one answer bring yet more questions? Does another answer shut down the conversation? Tweak your answers until you know which types of answer will intrigue your audience.

REFINE, REPEAT, REFINE, REPEAT

Your elevator pitch should be so ingrained in your head that, without even thinking, you can immediately and intuitively answer the question "What does (your company name) do?" Say the pitch to yourself over and over and over again, and find excuses to say it to others, even if they don't exactly ask that question. You should also have your co-founders and first employees memorize your elevator pitch. At random times, just ask them what your company does and see if they've got at least the first sentence of the pitch memorized.

As your company evolves, so should your elevator pitch. The most compelling thing you do could change over time and your most compelling "so what?" claims will certainly change. If not, you have bigger problems than a stagnant elevator pitch.

VARIATIONS FOR DIFFERENT AUDIENCES

You can use your elevator pitch with a variety of different audiences. The most common will be investors and prospective customers.

Because of this, you will likely end up with multiple versions. The good news is that the basic foundation and much of the messaging will be identical across all versions. The differences will mostly be tweaks that are easy to remember.

Regarding investors, understand that a great elevator pitch alone won't get you funded; it's just a door opener to a longer conversation. You've got to be fundable to get funded. However, I will say that a crappy elevator pitch can severely impact your ability to get funded even if you are truly fundable. In other words, a great elevator pitch can be a prerequisite to having the needed follow-on conversations with an investor prospect.

PITCH DECKS

In the old days, we actually wrote out a 20 to 30-page business plan document. Today, a tool called a *pitch deck* serves as a summarized and visual version of a business plan. It is in the form of a slide presentation and will become the single most valuable communication tool to use with audiences of all types. You will rely on it for multiple purposes. You'll use it for presentations to investors, and if you ever decide to pitch at a formal pitching event, you'll obviously need one. You can also use it as a supporting visual backdrop for sit-down conversations with investors.

The absolute most important aspect of an effective pitch deck is the storyline that serves as the foundation. Second most important is the flow (topic order) and content. Formatting is also important, but if the prior-mentioned ingredients aren't right, formatting alone won't save you.

FOUNDATION

A great pitch deck takes the audience on a journey. It should be like a story—compelling and with a beginning, middle, and end. After hearing the story, you want the audience to be interested in more information, ask more questions, and draw certain desired conclusions.

Those desired conclusions should be identified ahead of time so they can serve as the foundation for your pitch deck; you'll build your story backward from these. Before worrying about the order of the slides and certainly before typing words onto the slides, first decide what you want the audience to conclude regarding your venture. That's your foundation, and both the content and flow of your pitch deck should be optimized to support it.

What sort of things might you want the audience to conclude? Below are some examples that might apply to your venture:

- This company's market opportunity is HUGE.
- That's a really innovative solution for a really nasty problem.
- These founders are total badass ninjas.
- Wow, they've already got some unbelievable traction.

What is most exciting about your business plan from an investor's perspective, and what conclusions are you hoping they will draw? As you tell your story using your pitch deck, you should put extra emphasis on the sections that specifically correspond to those same topics. This means extra slides, extra content, and extra time spent on those sections to help ensure the desired conclusion is reached.

FLOW

The sequence of topics in your pitch must support the objective of creating a compelling story. There are multiple ways any given story can be told, but for fundraising purposes, there is a common pitch deck flow that active investors are used to seeing. I will explain that sequence as a starting point while also covering the typical content that is included with each section. The guidance provided here assumes you have a shipping product with paying customers. If you haven't yet launched your product, in some sections, you will instead discuss your plans, projections, and predictions, while other sections (or subsections) might need to be skipped altogether for now.

THE PROBLEM

What problem does your solution solve? Every section in your pitch deck is important, but this one is absolutely critical. If the investor doesn't believe you are solving a problem that needs to be solved or that isn't sufficiently painful to cause people to pay money to have it solved, you may as well stop the meeting. That's because the rest of your business plan doesn't matter.

Storytelling is often a great way to convey the problem you're solving. Describe either a real or mythical customer in the context of the problem. Set the stage with some background about them or their situation and then transition into the problem they experience. If you or someone close to you has experienced the problem, then tell your own story. This has the added benefit of evidencing your personal passion for the company's mission.

The nastier the investor perceives the problem to be, the better. Here's a brief example for a mythical company named DoggieDrone:

This is Florence. She's 84 years old and lives at home by herself. Not only does she enjoy the company of her dog, Sunny, but her doctor told her that having a loving pet at home helps keep her blood pressure down and her depression in check.

The problem is Florence's health no longer allows her to take Sunny for the walks outside that he really enjoys and gains exercise from. It really saddens her when Sunny paws at the front door to signal that he's ready for a walk outside. Sometimes she actually pays a neighbor kid to take Sunny for a walk, but that cost really adds up for two walks per day, and the neighbor isn't even available that often.

Figure 4.1. The problem DoggieDrone solves

I'll stop there because hopefully you get the idea of how storytelling can both explain the problem you're solving and help the investor actually feel the pain of your customer. Don't you feel bad for Florence, and don't you want to help her and Sunny? Now just imagine the story you could tell if the problem solved is brain cancer or cyberterrorism.

You don't have to tell a story, but you must convey the problem you solve in such a way that the investor both understands and identifies with the pain. With this, you will have their full attention for the next section of your pitch.

THE MARKET

The second crucial part is your opportunity to describe the audience or audiences that most experience the problem you solve. What do your target customers have in common? Perhaps they're in the same industry or have similar demographics.

This is also your opportunity to communicate the size of your market. How big would you be if you sold your product to every constituent that needs it? This is called your total available market (TAM). There are other variations of market sizing, and you'll need to educate yourself on this to make sure you don't lose credibility with the investor. It is also important that they see you serving a big market. That usually means having a TAM in excess of $1 billion.

The DoggieDrone pitch deck might mention the 30 million families worldwide that have one or more pet dogs. Assuming a $500 purchase price, DoggieDrone's TAM is $15 billion (30 million x $500). But maybe the first version of the drone only supports dogs up to 25 pounds and is only sold in the United States. This information is used to determine the current serviceable market (called SAM). And maybe their product roadmap has plans for a mobile app that will be sold via subscription, which will affect the future TAM and SAM in a positive way.

This is also the section where you can describe other interesting attributes about the market you serve. Is it growing rapidly? Are there any interesting trends that relate to your solution or business model? Is it highly fragmented and available for entry? Educate the investor about your market in ways that best support your vision and business plan.

$15 Billion Market Size (TAM)

30 million families worldwide own pet dogs

$1.2 trillion is spent annually on pet products

The elderly population is the fastest growing market

Figure 4.2. DoggieDrone's market

THE SOLUTION

The solution is what founders love to talk about the most. Just remember that investors want to see that you're building a viable and highly scalable *company*, not just a product. As you describe your solution offering, focus more on the benefits it provides users than on the features and capabilities it incorporates. It's OK to show what the product looks like, but don't turn your whole investor pitch into a product demo.

The DoggieDrone pitch deck would focus on how easy it is to select a walking distance and desired route, see real-time video of the dog on a walk, and calculate the estimated time remaining for the walk. It would have a sexy image of the product in action, but it would not include a bunch of technical specifications for the drone.

If you have any patents or technological characteristics that could be considered unfair advantages against the competition, this is the place to cover that information. In fact, investors will at least want to understand the competitive landscape you're playing in. A four-quadrant diagram is usually most effective, with your company in the top-right quadrant. You get to decide what the axes represent. If this doesn't work for you, consider a multicolumn checklist, with your company as the first or last column, or a Venn diagram, with your company at the intersection in the middle. The purpose of sharing your competitive positioning isn't to get into the weeds on tactical details but rather to support the high-level story you're telling the investor. It is not only OK to show that you have competition, but it's expected. "We don't have any competition" is immediately met with skepticism on the part of the investors, even though every once in a while it's true.

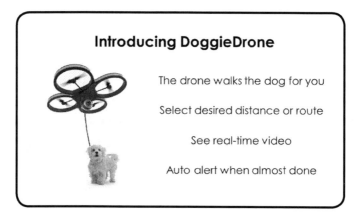

Figure 4.3. DoggieDrone's solution

THE BUSINESS MODEL

Your business model is composed of two key things: how you acquire customers and how you make money. For customer acquisition, don't get into details about specific marketing campaigns, but rather describe the various methods you use for acquiring customers. Maybe in order to get paying customers, your business model incorporates a combination of a free entry-level offer (called a "freemium") and self-service fulfillment. Or maybe you have a network of distribution partners that sell your product. DoggieDrone probably sells both online and in retail pet supply stores.

For making money, you should describe how your product is priced and any information you have about average transaction size or similar metrics that relate to monetization. This is also a good section to describe the most important metrics that make up your unit economics.

DEFINITION: UNIT ECONOMICS

Unit economics is the science of breaking your business into individual units of measure related to the specific activities that ultimately lead to revenue. The activities and related metrics typically span the customer acquisition lifecycle, starting with awareness to consideration and finally to a decision. Unique elements of unit economics are associated with each of the various possible startup business models.

Figure 4.4. DoggieDrone's business model

TRACTION

Any evidence that your business model is (or will be) viable can be considered traction. Of course, a trend graph showing aggressive growth of paying customers is the best form of traction, but it is not the only one. If you haven't yet launched, you'll need to get creative in order to evidence traction. Preorders are nice. Active trials or letters of intent to purchase are better than nothing. A signed strategic partnership that isn't yet producing results but seems very promising will carry some traction value. Even things like awards, positive influencer reviews, and press coverage can carry a little traction weight until you are generating revenue.

Figure 4.5. Evidence of DoggieDrone's traction

YOUR TEAM

Investors are betting on you and your team above everything else. A strong team will adjust and adapt, as necessary, until a great company with a great business model is identified. Share key insights about the skills, backgrounds, and success record of key team members, especially proof points that directly relate to the current opportunity. This section can include board members or advisors if they bring something special to the table and can boost the credibility of the team. In the early days, when there are only a couple of founders, this can be especially helpful.

For example, DoggieDrone's CEO previously founded a company that made the world's first automatic dog and cat feeder system and later sold the company to the largest manufacturer of pet supplies for $350 million. They also have an advisory board member that is the current chairman of the largest pet store retailer in the country.

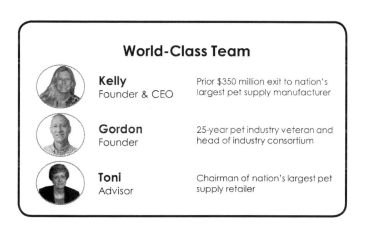

Figure 4.6. The DoggieDrone team

THE CALL TO ACTION

You are asking for an investment, right? This is the section where you share important details about your funding round. It typically includes the target funding amount, a couple of key investment terms, and the outcomes you expect to accomplish with the desired funding. Focus on outcomes, not the activities you will engage in or the ways you will spend the money. Remember that investors write checks for outcomes, not activities.

The $2 million that DoggieDrone is raising for their seed round is expected to enable them to create a second model of the drone that supports dogs that weigh between 25 and 50 pounds, which expands their serviceable market by 125%. It also enables them to ramp up to 550 unit sales per month, reduce their manufacturing costs by 20% due to the increased volume, and improve their gross profit margins from 50% to 60%. Those are great outcomes for an investor to fund.

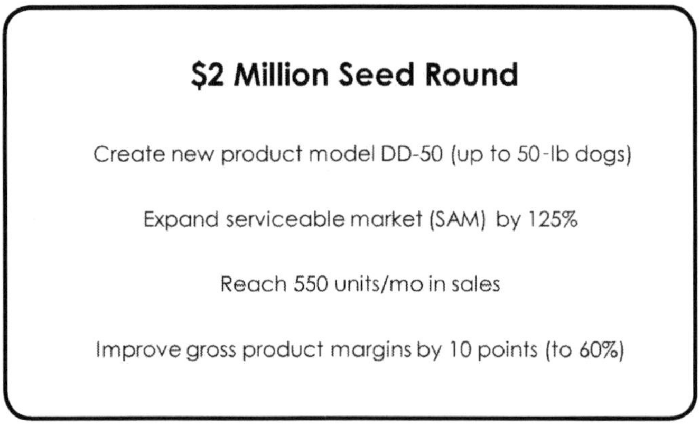

Figure 4.7. DoggieDrone's fundraising call to action

THE BACKUP SECTION

The backup section will become one of your greatest assets. It sits after the call-to-action slide and serves as a repository of information to support Q&A. You can't possibly fit every aspect of your business plan in the main part of the pitch deck. You also don't know what questions or objections each investor will have; but if you have a slide in the backup section for each of the things you don't want included in the main section, you can jump there to help answer specific questions or alleviate concerns.

Charts and graphs, more product screen shots or diagrams, your product roadmap, detailed financial projections, and the like can make for great backup section content. In fact, you will probably find that your backup section grows as you meet with more and more investors and discover the most common questions and objections that would benefit from having a backup slide.

If you are ever required to email the pitch deck to a prospective investor before a first meeting, you might want to remove the backup section. I say "required" because your objective is to get a face-to-face meeting. You don't want them to make their full decision based on your emailed pitch deck alone. But after politely pushing back on the request and offering a second time to buy the investor coffee, you might get a reaction that causes you to realize that emailing your pitch deck is the only way to keep the opportunity alive.

THE FULL STORYLINE

In a highly simplified narrative form, the final result of this suggested flow might be something like this:

> There is this really significant ***problem*** in a huge ***market***. We developed an ideal and unique ***solution***, figured out an efficient method of making money ***(business model)***, and have evidence ***(traction)*** to validate that our business plan and long-range vision are sound. We've assembled the perfect ***team*** and just need $750,000 ***(call to action)*** to achieve our next significant set of milestones and continue to pursue global world domination and make you a lot of money in return.

Like with any template, your company's pitch deck version will vary. If the experience and credentials of your team are among your biggest selling points, then you might want to cover the team first, even before describing the problem you're solving. Imagine the starting reaction of an investor if you tell them this is your third startup, all with exits, and the most recent one provided a 20X financial return to your investors. There's no reason to leave information like that till the end of your pitch.

KEEP IT SIMPLE

Notice that you didn't see a suggested section in the pitch deck for detailed financial projections. That is because it is a separate tool on its own. For prelaunch startups, I don't think a financial projection slide in the main section of the deck is required, because it's total guesswork. For startups with an early track record of revenue and projecting $1 million or more over the next year, a financial projection slide probably generates credibility and helps support a needed dialogue about the future. But any projection slide in the main portion of the deck should only have high-level information, perhaps communicated via a graph. More detail about your financial projections can be put in the backup section. And regardless of where you put this information in your pitch deck, don't project out five years. Startups seeking a seed round of funding can project 18 to 24 months of financials, while those seeking a Series A might need to project out three years.

MULTIPLE VERSIONS

You will need at least two versions of your pitch deck: one for 5-minute onstage pitch competitions and another that is longer and used for in-person investor meetings. Most sections will only have one or two slides. This means the onstage pitch version probably has 8 to 10 slides total, and the sit-down version with investors probably has 12 to 15 slides plus a backup section. Furthermore, a pitch deck for Series-A funding is typically a little longer than one for a seed round, and that's because there is more information to cover—more traction, more interesting metrics, more customers and partners, bigger team size, and so on. But your objective is not to jam as much information as possible into the pitch deck but rather to have the right information to help tell your story and facilitate an exciting dialogue.

TEST-DRIVING THE PITCH DECK

Just like your elevator pitch, your pitch deck should be practiced with a friendly audience, then repeatedly refined. If you were to put version numbers on your pitch deck to track the iterations and evolution over time, you might literally end up with 30 versions or more by the time the funding round is closed. This is because the reactions you get from many investor meetings will cause you to realize that some key points aren't clear, some are causing unnecessary concern, or a change needs to be made to the sequence of slides to better support storytelling.

The best way to fine-tune your pitch deck in the early days of its use is to take it out on a test-drive. First, with friends and family as purely penalty-free practices. Then try it out on mentors at the incubator where you work or random investors that exhibit low odds of investing in your venture. Basically, you want to iterate and improve quite a bit before using the pitch deck with the best, high-value investors on your prospect list. Your pitch deck will continue to iterate, even after using it with these high-value investors, but at least you won't embarrass yourself or kill the deal just because of a crappy pitch deck.

PITCHING EVENTS

One of the tools in your fundraising toolkit isn't a piece of content but rather an activity you can participate in to get exposure to investors and prospective customers. I'm talking about pitching events such as the popular demo day. Not only do investors attend these events, but many of them include a cash award for the winner. That all sounds like a form of fundraising to me, and these events are so prevalent that you will want to be prepared to participate before an opportunity is announced.

Before your first formal pitching event, you probably had only two rehearsed modes of responding to interested investors: your short elevator pitch and a pitch deck for a 30- to 45-minute investor meeting. Preparing for a pitching event forces you to tell the most important elements of your story in three to five minutes.

You will rehearse the onstage pitch so many times that it will forever be committed to memory. A side benefit of this will become clear during future meetings with interested investors. When they ask how big your market is, your immediate mental reaction will be "That's slide 3," and when they ask how you plan to make money, "That's slide 7." Your best explanations will already be on the tip of your tongue.

Although the story you will tell during a demo-day pitch is generally the same as during an in-person meeting with an investor, there is one big difference. You will be standing in front of an audience, and maybe even a large audience of hundreds. If you aren't comfortable or experienced with such a setting, the only way to get better is to practice. Start by practicing in front of friends and family, then try to find a pitching event that typically draws a small audience of 20 to 30 people. The more you practice in front of a crowd, the more comfortable you will get.

PREPARATION

Too often, I see startup founders make basic mistakes that could have easily been avoided if they had prepared, even just a little. I actually think it's a common personality trait of many entrepreneurs. They take pride in being able to wing it. But if the stakes are high, why impose the extra risk? Instead, be prepared.

TO MEMORIZE OR NOT TO MEMORIZE

It is actually a personal decision whether to memorize your onstage pitch. I always recommend that presenters memorize—at a minimum—the opening statement, closing statement, and select key message points in between. It is also true that shorter pitches of three minutes are easier to memorize than those of five minutes or longer.

Regardless of how much of your pitch you decide to memorize, I recommend using trigger words—key phrases that cue your memory. The images and text on your slides can obviously help you, but you don't want to always have to turn your head and look at the slides just to remember what you want to say. Instead, think of a key word or short phrase that is in the first sentence of your narrative for that slide. On the typed-out version of your pitch, highlight those trigger words in a different color so that as you are practicing, the trigger words easily jump off the page and eventually sink into your brain. You'll be amazed how often during later practices without the written script you will be able to mentally visualize the highlighted trigger words to launch the narrative for each slide. If you ever get stuck, just think about the trigger word.

SUPPORTED PRESENTATION FORMATS

Pay attention to the information packet you receive to prepare you for the event. It likely includes information about what is allowed and what isn't. The first is the file format. You will need to submit your presentation in a format such as PowerPoint, Keynote, or PDF. If PowerPoint or Keynote is allowed, don't use a nonstandard font but rather go with one of the common ones that are natively supported by these programs. Your presentation is going to get loaded onto someone else's computer, and if they don't have the same fonts you used, crazy things can happen onscreen, and you won't catch it until you're on the stage, staring at an audience of 100 people.

If only PDF is allowed, any animations you configured into your PowerPoint or Keynote presentation will be lost. I'm referring to things like animated movement of progressive revealing of an onslide image, graphic, or text. If this type of animation is important, here's a trick. Create successive slides, each with an incremental change. That way, as you advance through the slides it gives the appearance of the most basic forms of animation. Of course, true motion can't be recreated, but appearance, disappearance, movement, and accentuation forms of animation are easy to replicate with this trick.

If you want to incorporate audio or video into your presentation, you should first understand that you are taking on additional risk. In my experience, 20% of the time some glitch happens to the audio or video while onstage. Make sure the multimedia setup for the pitch event will support the audio or video format you are using.

YOUR SLIDES

If you already have a pitch deck for use when meeting investors, you've got a great start for your onstage pitch deck. The flow of information will be the same, but you might need to remove some slides and even entire sections, depending on the maximum allowed length of the pitch. The key changes you'll need to make relate to the differences with an onstage pitch in front of an audience.

First, you'll want to review the font sizes on each slide. If your slide content can only be read by people in the first few rows, your ideal billionaire investor sitting in row 18 won't get all the information she needs to decide if you're the startup she wants to talk to during the break. What a missed opportunity! When in doubt, go larger on text size. Test it yourself by standing eight feet away from your laptop while navigating through your presentation in slide show mode. Can you easily read everything? Try again while standing 20 feet away from a 42-inch monitor.

Second, you don't want a bunch of narrative text on the slides. You want the audience looking at and listening to you, not reading the slides. Use the fewest number of words possible, and leave a lot of white space on the slides. For example, if your market size is $3.5 billion, the slide might literally just show "$3.5B" in huge text right in the middle of the slide. No title, no other narrative—just the number. Another trick is to use images to fill the complete slide. Again, you want the audience listening to what you have to say. The slides should simply complement your narrative, not overtake it.

PRACTICE, PRACTICE, PRACTICE

I know, you hated it when your parents said "Practice makes perfect," but you're going to hear it again from me. Whether you choose to memorize your pitch or not, you want to practice at least 50 times before the actual event, and 100 times is even better, especially if you decide to memorize. Another objective of repeated practice is to get the timing down to fit within the allowed time, so make sure to time yourself until you're consistently on your mark.

While practicing, don't just barely go through the motions; practice as often as possible as if you are actually onstage. I'm referring to your pace of speech, level of excitement, voice inflections, short pauses for effect, hand gestures, and periodic visual glances to the left and right side of the imaginary audience. This might seem awkward and embarrassing, but it basically develops the needed "muscle memory" to help your live pitch incorporate these same attributes. In fact, make sure to practice in front of an audience (even a small one) as often as possible, because that's closer to what you'll experience during the real event. They can also give you feedback about content, delivery, and style. If doing these mock pitch practices makes you uncomfortable, great. It's better to experience being uncomfortable in front of small audiences of people you know and starting to get used to it than experiencing it for the first time in front of an audience of 100.

PREPARE FOR QUESTIONS

If your pitching event calls for a Q&A session with assigned panelists or judges immediately after your pitch, prepare for the questions you might get. If you've been in fundraising mode and have been meeting with investors, you are likely to have heard 90% of all possible questions, with the most common ones over and over. But while you may have plenty of time to answer questions during investor meetings, that's not the case while onstage. Therefore, your answers should be compelling, clear, and concise. Shoot for 10 to 15 seconds ideally, because it optimizes for cycling through more questions. This gives the best opportunity to expose other interesting aspects of your business that you couldn't fit into the pitch. Write down a list of the 10 to 20 common questions you should expect, and make notes of a compelling, clear, and concise answer for each. You don't need to memorize the answers; just be prepared for how you want to answer.

JUDGES

If your event calls for judges, you must do some additional research ahead of time. What criteria will they use to decide on the award? Use this to influence the content, flow, and delivery of your pitch. What is each judge's background? Find their biography (their LinkedIn profile is usually fine) to determine how much they might know about your industry, product, or business model, then predict what questions they might ask.

THE DAY OF THE EVENT

By this time, you're well rehearsed and ready for any curveball questions the judges can possibly throw at you, but there's still more you can do to have the best pitch possible. The objective is to eliminate as many surprises and first-time experiences as possible so you can just concentrate on telling your story and connecting with the audience. Get into the conference room as early as allowed to see the size, shape, and audience layout. Stand on the stage to determine exactly where you will be positioned, where the presentation screen is, and what the atmosphere looks like from there.

Is there a smaller monitor in front of the stage that you will be able to look at as a reference during your presentation (called a *confidence monitor*)? Where will the judges or panelists be sitting, and how should you be oriented when taking their questions versus presenting to the audience?

Ask the coordinator of the event to show you the handheld remote clicker you will use to advance the slides. Hold it in your hand and click the forward and backward buttons to get a feel. Find out if you'll be using a wireless mic attached to your shirt or a handheld one. If it's a handheld, hold the microphone in your hand to see how it feels, and imagine what it will be like to have a mic in one hand and a clicker in the other.

If you have embedded audio or video in your presentation, beg the organizer to give it a test using the actual A/V setup that is being used. You don't want onstage surprises. And if you're a paranoid type like me, transfer a copy of your presentation to a memory stick and take it with you as an emergency backup. Have it in multiple formats (i.e., PowerPoint and PDF or Keynote and PDF).

FINANCIAL PROJECTION MODEL

We previously talked about financial projections in the context of what might be included in your pitch deck. But that's just a high-level summary of your projections and is usually focused on revenue growth. Investors want to know that you've projected your financial future in more detail and that you understand the underpinnings of your projection model.

In fact, I initially ignore the actual numbers that result from the projection model. Instead, I first want to see if the founder actually understands how the model works and which metrics provide the most leverage. If someone else put together your financial model using your input, make sure they explain every last detail, and make sure to experiment with the various knobs and levers within the model to understand their effects. You will be quizzed deeply by some investors. And you don't get credit for just *having* a financial model; you have to understand and defend it.

Startups in the pre-seed funding stage don't need a sophisticated financial model and don't need to project out more than about 18 months. The focus should be on the projected profit and loss (P&L) because it shows both revenue growth and the expected net loss over time. With each subsequent funding stage, the model needs a longer projection, more detail, more input variables to experiment with, and generally more sophistication. A Series A funding round will project out three years and probably also require a cash flow projection, since net loss and cash consumption often deviate from each other.

Remember that financial results are derived from operational outcomes. For example, a startup with a self-service business model might encourage website visitors to download a freemium version of their product and then nurture those users in a way that convinces a subset of them to upgrade to the paid version of the product. Operational metrics like monthly website visitors, the ratio of freemium downloads, and conversion rates to the paid version are critical for this company and, therefore, should be incorporated as inputs in the financial projection model. Believe me when I predict that you will become an absolute ninja with your operational and financial model as a result of the fundraising process.

SUMMARIZING STARTUP SUCCESS

Your key fundraising tools will be created during the strategy and planning phases, so not only do you have them by the time your campaign officially begins, but also they'll have already gone through some refinement. You'll need to create a financial projection model during the strategy phase in order to determine the right amount of funding to raise, and you'll need at least early versions of your pitch deck to support your investor interactions during all of the planning phases.

You've noticed that the suggested pitch deck sections cover all key aspects of your business plan, not just your product. Many startup founders are so focused on the product they are creating that they forget that investors invest money to build companies—hopefully scalable and sustainable ones—not products. The product is very important, but only in context of the grander business you're building around it.

Your elevator pitch, pitch deck, and financial model will serve as your foundational fundraising tools, and that's why I covered each of them in so much detail. Beyond that, you will almost certainly develop additional tools to best support your campaign. One example is a monthly update template for allowing interested investors to monitor your progress and, thereby, keep them warm. If you send those updates like clockwork every month and give an honest picture of the company's accomplishments and issues, you'll also earn needed respect and credibility with investors.

Another example is a one-page executive summary of your company and investment opportunity (called a *one-pager*). You will find numerous templates to consider and might find that it is the best piece of collateral to send an inquiring investor rather than your whole pitch deck. Remember, you want to present your pitch deck in person whenever possible.

If you follow the various recommendations and best practices that we have covered so far, you will be better prepared than 90% of the hundreds of startup founders I work with every year. Strategy set? Check. Battle plans ready? Check. Tools sharpened? Check. Great, let's figure out the best fundraising instrument to use and then go fill up your bank account with investors' money.

 AHA MOMENTS

1. Your elevator pitch only needs to accomplish one thing—cause the other party to ask *any* question so that you can continue the conversation.

2. An effective elevator pitch describes what the company does and why someone should care. Usually, that can be conveyed in two sentences.

3. You might end up with a couple of variations of your elevator pitch to be used with uniquely different audiences.

4. All employees during the early days should memorize the elevator pitch.

5. Pitch decks should take the audience on a journey.

6. The foundation of your pitch deck is your key desired conclusions. Identify them first and make sure they are accentuated.

7. Your fundraising call-to-action slide should focus on the outcomes you will achieve with the funding rather than planned activities or how you will spend the money.

8. The backup section of the pitch deck will become your best friend during times of investor Q&A.

9. Practice makes perfect for onstage pitching events. Do so in role-playing mode as often as possible.

10. Spend extra time preparing for pitching events to eliminate last-minute surprises. Read the guidelines they send ahead of time, and ask questions when in doubt.

11. Your financial projection model is something you must understand well enough to defend with a probing and skeptical investor.

CHAPTER 5

DEMYSTIFYING CONVERTIBLE SECURITIES

"Simplicity is the ultimate sophistication."

—Leonardo da Vinci

There are a variety of fundraising strategies and associated vehicles to use for pre-seed and seed rounds of funding. You can seek traditional debt, but you will probably be required to give a personal guarantee (yikes!). You might be able to apply for a government grant or launch a presales campaign on one of the popular crowdfunding portals. You might even offer investors what's called *revenue-based funding* (RBF), in which you pay them a percentage of either revenue or profit until they've received an agreed multiple of their investment.

You could sell equity in your company, but investors rarely want the same *common* class of shares that you and the other employees were issued. They want a special class, called *preferred* shares, which come with all sorts of special rights. But during your very early days, you don't want to grant a bunch of special rights, you aren't quite prepared to set an exact valuation for your company, and you won't want to pay the high legal costs that usually accompany an equity round of funding.

None of the prior-mentioned funding vehicles are as popular as convertible securities for seed rounds of funding up to about $1 million and sometimes considerably more. That's because of their ease of use, flexibility, and low associated legal costs. Due to their popularity, you need to understand how convertible securities work, how to administer them, and when to use them to your best advantage. You should also understand the most sensitive issues from the investor's perspective.

CONVERSION BASICS

As the name suggests, convertible securities are intended to *convert* into something, and that something is equity. Most investors want equity in your company and are willing to invest now while waiting until certain conditions are suitable to actually get that equity. More specifically, they are willing to wait until they can get a preferred class of equity.

At a basic level, convertible securities are simple. They convert an investor's invested capital into preferred equity once you create and sell that class of shares to future investors in an equity round of funding. With this, investors in both the early and later rounds of funding end up with the same preferred shareholder rights. But even though the basics of convertible security mechanics are simple, the devil is in the details. Let's start with the standard terms for most forms of convertible securities.

DEFINITION: CLASSES OF STOCK

There are typically two broad classes of stock created over time. Before taking on external funding, most startups only have what is referred to as *common* stock. But later, when professional investors put money into the company, they want special rights for economic protection and an element of protectionary control. These extra rights define a new class of shares referred to as *preferred* shares. In this way, a *class* of stock denotes a group of shareholders with the same rights. Sometimes this results in multiple subclasses of shares being created to further differentiate the rights of a larger class. In other words, a company might have Series Seed Preferred, Series A-1 Preferred, and Series A-2 Preferred classes of stock, each with a different set of rights, even if only slightly different. In fact, just using the word "Series" to denote a share class almost always indicates it is a preferred class of stock.

DISCOUNT

It's not fair that the early investors get their equity at the same valuation as the future investors. After all, the money from the early investors comes at a time when the company's viability is riskier. Their early investment facilitates company growth and other valuation-driving milestones along the way to the future equity round of funding that will trigger the conversion. One way to compensate for this is to give the early investors a discount against the future valuation before calculating how much equity they will get.

A 20% discount is by far the most typical for pre-seed and seed stage funding rounds. With this, if you were to negotiate a $5 million pre-money valuation for your future equity-based funding round, the holders of convertible securities will, instead, get equity based on a $4 million valuation (20% discount applied to $5 million). This means that, on a dollar-for-dollar basis, they will get more equity than the future investors, and that's absolutely fair.

VALUATION CAP

What if the investments from the early-stage investors allow the company to fly like a rocket ship and reach a future valuation of something like $20 million when they raise their first equity-based funding round? It seems hugely unfair that the early investors convert to equity at a $16 million valuation (assuming a 20% discount). There is no way the two parties would have been discussing such a high valuation if they had been forced to when the prior investment was made. To offset this risk and protect the early investors, most convertible securities include what's called a *valuation cap* (a.k.a. the *cap*).

Using an example of a $4 million cap and a 20% discount, if the company is able to raise an equity round of funding from future investors at a pre-money valuation greater than $5 million, the early investors' investments convert to equity, assuming the valuation was only $4 million (the cap). In this way, the investors get either the discounted valuation or the valuation cap amount, whichever is more favorable to them. Using the prior-mentioned example, any future valuation less than $5 million will result in the discount being applied (since it yields a conversion valuation less than the $4 million cap), and any future valuation higher than $5 million would result in the valuation cap being used (since all of these scenarios otherwise would yield a valuation more than the $4 million cap if the discount were applied).

Refer to figure 5.1 below to make sure you're clear on the relationship between the discount and the valuation cap. In this scenario, the convertible note has a $4 million valuation cap and a 20% discount. What you see are three different equity conversion scenarios, each with a different pre-money valuation for the equity round of funding (a Series A in this case) that causes the notes to convert to equity.

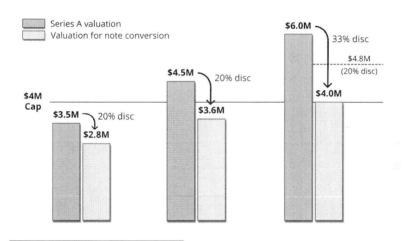

Figure 5.1. Note conversion examples

$3.5 MILLION VALUATION

Applying the 20% discount yields a $2.8 million result; since that is *below* the $4 million valuation cap, the note holders convert to equity using a $2.8 million valuation.

$4.5 MILLION VALUATION

Although the Series A valuation is higher than the cap, applying the 20% discount yields a $3.6 million result. Since that is *below* the $4 million valuation cap, the note holders convert to equity using a $3.6 million valuation.

$6.0 MILLION VALUATION

Applying the 20% discount yields a $4.8 million result; since that is *above* the $4 million valuation cap, the note holders convert to equity using the $4 million valuation.

ADDITIONAL CONSIDERATIONS

With just the information provided in these examples, we aren't able to determine the exact amount of equity the note holders will get. That is due to other factors, such as the ultimate post-money valuation when the equity round closes and other required actions that could affect the cap table with the equity round of funding.

When convertible securities convert to equity using the valuation cap, we can also calculate the *effective* discount as a benchmark. For example, using the figure above with a $4 million cap, a future equity valuation of $6 million yields an effective 33% discount for the early investors that invested using a convertible security ($4 million is 33% lower than $6 million). If, instead, the future valuation is $20 million, the effective discount jumps to 80%.

Setting the cap excessively low, even for just a subset of your pre-seed or seed investors, can cause big issues upon conversion to equity. When I say "excessively low," I mean a cap that could yield an effective discount in excess of 70%. This scenario gives the early investors such an excessive economic advantage and associated excessive amount of equity that the lead investor for the equity round of funding might not be able to reach their required equity target. That can be a deal killer. But it also depends on how much investment, in total, converts at an excessively high discount. A single investor in a very early round with only a $25,000 investment might not cause a big problem. But a full $500,000 seed round at that level will surely cause a problem.

It is not required to include a valuation cap with your convertible security. Experienced investors will definitely take note if you don't, and it might prevent them from investing. But if your investment opportunity is highly sought after, you might be able to get away with what's called an *uncapped* convertible security. Just know that it's extremely rare.

EARLY EXIT MULTIPLE

What if the company skyrockets and ends up being acquired for a decent amount of money before ever needing to raise an equity round of funding that would cause the conversion? It seems unfair that the early investors only get their initial investment back. In order to reward the early investors, many convertible securities have rights related to such a change-of-control event that call for the investor to get some multiple of their invested capital.

DEFINITION: CHANGE OF CONTROL

An activity that causes a change of company ownership is considered a change of control. An outright acquisition is the most familiar form, but other actions that significantly affect the balance of equity ownership can also be considered a change of control, depending on the definition included in the legal document.

A 2X multiple is fairly common for this, and it allows the early investors to double their invested amount. Some convertible securities also give the investor an option to instead convert to equity using the stated valuation cap as the valuation. If that gives them a better return than the exit multiple, they can participate in the acquisition as an equity holder with others.

SIMULATING FUTURE CONVERSION

Due to the interaction of various terms included with both the early-stage convertible security and the future equity round of funding that causes their conversion, it's difficult to predict what the future cap table will look like after conversions. That means it's also hard to explain to a casual, early-stage investor how much equity they might end up with in the future. The good news is there are plenty of online cap table simulators (including one on the resources page of my website) to help you run various scenarios and eliminate the guesswork.

CONVERTIBLE NOTES

The most popular form of convertible security for early-stage startup funding is the convertible note (a.k.a. "note"). As the word *note* suggests, it is a form of debt (a loan). But instead of making regular payments to pay off the debt, the principal amount of the note plus accrued interest over time converts to equity when an equity round of funding is raised and using the mechanics previously described. And since convertible notes are a form of debt, they include a couple of unique terms.

TERM (MATURITY DATE)

Just like a car loan or a home mortgage, convertible notes have a stated term and associated maturity date (the end of the term). If you reach the maturity date without a natural conversion to equity, the note holder could technically call for you to immediately pay back their principal amount plus accrued interest. This is referred to as *calling the note*. But since that would likely kill an early-stage company, there are usually some other options.

Upon approaching the end of the term, it's not unusual for a startup to ask for an extension to the maturity date. Some convertible notes even give the early investor an option to convert to common class equity if the maturity date is reached. They do so by using the valuation cap or a discounted version of the valuation cap to determine how much equity they get. I find that, as long as a reasonable valuation cap is in place to protect the investor, and as long as the company still has decent odds of raising an equity round of funding, most investors are OK to grant an extension to the maturity date. They will continue to accrue interest and are still hoping to get a preferred class of stock for their investment.

Make sure to give yourself enough time via the stated term when using a convertible note. A term of 18 to 24 months is typical for a seed round, and 36 months shouldn't be frowned upon for a pre-seed round. You basically need enough time to safely reach an equity round of funding in which you sell a preferred class of shares to future investors.

INTEREST RATE

Like any form of debt, convertible notes carry an interest rate. The interest accrues until either an equity conversion takes place or the note is paid off. For the conversion to equity, the amount of accrued interest is added to the investment principal before calculating how much equity the investor gets. In other words, a $50,000 note investment might later convert to equity at a total value in the $53,000 to $58,000 range, depending on the interest rate and how much time goes by before conversion.

Early investors aren't investing just to earn interest on their investment. But that doesn't mean they won't notice a ridiculously low interest rate. Most of the notes I see offer an interest rate in the 6% to 8% range. If you stick within that range, you probably won't get any pushback from investors.

QUALIFIED FINANCING (A.K.A. QUALIFYING TRANSACTION)

Most convertible notes don't convert to equity unless the future equity round of funding reaches a stated minimum size. A term commonly called *qualified financing* defines this minimum amount. A typical qualified financing amount is two to three times the target size of the pre-seed or seed funding round. Technically speaking, if a future equity round of funding does not reach the minimum threshold, the note holders aren't entitled to an equity conversion.

COMPARING THE SAFE TO CONVERTIBLE NOTES

Initially made available by a world-renowned startup accelerator called Y Combinator (YC) in 2013, and subsequently updated in late 2018, the SAFE is a convertible security that was created to serve as an alternative to the highly popular convertible note. SAFE stands for *simple agreement for future equity*, and it is prevalent in California. Since its introduction, its use has spread throughout the country. At the time of this writing, SAFEs probably represent 20%

of early-stage investment rounds outside of California among those using convertible securities.

A SAFE is a short investment document that has been open-sourced and is intended to be simple to understand and convenient to administer. It's not a debt instrument, and that's mostly what makes it different from a convertible note. SAFEs don't have a maturity date or a stated interest rate. You can see a side-by-side comparison of the SAFE and convertible notes in figure 5.2 below.

Attribute	SAFE	C-Note
Convertible Security	✓	✓
Discount	✓	✓
Valuation Cap	✓	✓
SEC Characterization	like a warrant	debt
Future Conversion	post-money	pre-money
Term (Maturity Date)		✓
Interest Rate		✓

Figure 5.2. Comparing SAFE to convertible notes

Until the 2018 SAFE template updates by YC, I wouldn't have disqualified a personal investment opportunity that uses a SAFE, and I wouldn't push hard on a startup I advise to switch from a SAFE to a convertible note. However, with the 2018 update, I have a different opinion, and it relates to the switch from a pre-money to a post-money calculation for future equity conversion. Without getting into the technical details, this change alone makes the SAFE much less founder friendly if they are used for multiple rounds of funding before an eventual conversion to equity. That is because it gives a big antidilution feature to the investors versus convertible notes. The holders of common stock (i.e., founders, employees, advisors) take the extra dilution hit upon the SAFE's conversion to equity, assuming the post-money version of the SAFE is used.

I also predict some misunderstanding and perception issues related to the higher amount needed for a post-money valuation cap. For example, a convertible note with a $6 million valuation cap (pre-money) might yield the investor the same post-conversion equity as a SAFE with an $8 million valuation cap (post-money). But investors might initially perceive the SAFE's valuation cap as overpriced just by looking at the numbers and comparing across multiple investment opportunities.

The new post-money SAFE template does bring more clarity to early investors regarding the likely equity they will get in the future, but this seems to be at the risk of extra dilution for common stock-holders. If you choose to use the post-money version of the SAFE, discuss this with your attorney and model various scenarios using a cap table simulator—more specifically, one that can accommodate convertible securities that convert to equity based on a post-money valuation cap.

The lack of a maturity date on the SAFE is worth noting. That's because there is a possibility that it never converts to equity, and there's also nothing in the terms that calls for the investment to be repaid to the investor. This is the most typical concern I hear from investors about the SAFE. With a convertible note, approaching the maturity date forces a conversation between the company and the investor. With a SAFE, the startup could evolve into a small—but profitable—lifestyle business that pays the founders a handsome salary but never reaches the point of being able to exit via acquisition. Any investor with a SAFE could end up getting stuck with no path to an investment return—and no recourse, either.

SAFEs don't convey an interest rate. But since investors aren't overly excited with making 6%–8% on their investment while waiting for it to convert to equity, I don't find the lack of an interest rate as a major inhibitor.

Since SAFEs are not considered securitized debt, if things don't work out and you have to liquidate the company, SAFE investors might be further down the list to get any entitled distributions from the assets you liquidate. Convertible note holders sit higher in the pecking order, and this might also be on the mind of your early investors, especially those that have had seed-stage investments crash and burn.

The way the SAFE documents are written, any size of preferred equity round of funding will cause the SAFE investment to convert to equity. This is compared to most convertible notes that require the future equity round of funding to reach or exceed the minimum size required to be considered a qualified financing.

If your company is established as a limited liability company (LLC) and you prefer to use the SAFE for your early-stage funding rounds, check with your attorney first to make sure it is possible. There are conflicting opinions on this, and alterations to the template might be required.

HOW TO CHOOSE?

I believe it would be a fair assessment to conclude that the original pre-money SAFE is slightly favorable to the startup, the newer post-money SAFE is very favorable to the investor, and convertible notes are slightly favorable to the investor. But that's not the only factor to take into consideration when deciding which form of convertible security to use. You must also take familiarity into consideration.

I mentioned that, at the time of this writing, probably only 20% of early-stage investments outside of California use SAFEs. That means that casual angel investors in your city or region might have never seen one. If they've never used it before, they might not be willing to take the time to educate themselves on the differences, and they certainly might not be willing to pay their personal attorney to review it and explain it to them. Saying that "it's just like a convertible note but without a maturity date or interest rate" would be mostly true, but possibly not enough to overcome the concern.

A seed round of $500,000 or more can easily involve 15 to 20 individual angel investors. If 30% of the angels in your local market aren't comfortable using the SAFE, you're adding headwind to your funding round. Because of this risk, if you want to use the SAFE, during the phases of your fundraising campaign in which you're determining investor interest and later getting more specific with them and prioritizing accordingly, try to gauge each investor's familiarity with SAFEs and their willingness to invest using them.

EXTREME FLEXIBILITY

Convertible securities are unbelievably flexible. Although they are commonly used to support a pre-seed or seed round of funding, the agreement is directly between an individual investor and the company. Technically speaking, each investor could be presented with different terms. Doing so would create an administrative mess for the startup, especially when trying to figure out the equity conversion mechanics. But it can be done, and it presents some interesting advantages and opportunities.

One such advantage is referred to as a *rolling close*. As each investor commits by signing the convertible security, they can transfer their funds and you can immediately put them to work. Equity rounds of funding usually have one or more official close dates with minimum threshold amounts for being able to get your hands on the funds.

The rolling close is a double-edged sword. On one hand, being able to gain possession of funding as the commitments are made allows you to immediately put the increments of new capital to work. On the other hand, if the commitments are spread out over several months, it can create a hand-to-mouth scenario that never lets the company really make the intended investments and commitments. Because of this, I strongly recommend only increasing expenditures based on actual investments received and not based on the target amount for the funding round.

BRIDGING A GAP USING CONVERTIBLE SECURITIES

Most startups think of convertible securities only in the context of a pre-seed or seed round of funding. What they don't know is that these instruments are ideal for a bridge round to close a needed gap to the next logical round of funding. It is important to understand the differences and nuances when using convertible securities for this purpose.

Previously, we reviewed the difference between wanting and needing to raise money. Bridge rounds can be associated with each case. You might be running low on cash and *need* to raise money to reach the sweet spot investor criteria for the next round of funding. Conversely, you might have a big outcome on the near-term horizon and *want* to raise money so that you can safely accomplish that outcome to get an associated bump up in valuation before you start your fundraising campaign. In either case, a bridge round is specifically used to buy enough time to bridge the needed gap.

THE BENEFITS OF USING A CONVERTIBLE SECURITY

For the same reasons convertible securities are so popular for pre-seed and seed rounds of funding, they are also ideal for bridge rounds. You aren't forced to set a valuation for the company, you get the advantage of a rolling close, and legal costs and associated efforts are fairly minimal. But since this is a short-term bridge intended to just buy a little extra time, there are typically some differences from using a convertible security for a seed round.

TERM

If you're using a convertible note, the term should be short. In fact, if the note doesn't have a short term, then it doesn't support the messaging of it being used to bridge a gap. Something in the range of six months is typical, and anything close to one year starts to smell like another regular round of funding rather than a bridge. For this reason, using a SAFE for a bridge round might be more difficult to sell to investors. It doesn't have a term or maturity date.

DISCOUNT

With such a short expected lifespan, a bridge round can come with a lower discount than a full seed round of funding. Whereas 20% is a typical discount for a regular round, a 10% discount is more typical for bridge rounds. This makes sense if you associate the planned runway with the discount offered. The shorter the runway, the lower the discount.

Some investors might worry that you will open up another bridge round due to difficulty in raising the intended equity round of funding. To offset this risk, you can offer a *staggered discount*. If the convertible security converts within six months, the investor gets a 10% discount, and if it takes longer than that, they get a 20% discount.

VALUATION CAP

For bridge rounds, it's more practical than for regular rounds of funding to not have a cap, especially if you fit into the "want extra time" category instead of "need extra time." Remember, the valuation cap is intended to offer the investor a high-side valuation protection mechanism. With a short term like six months, the odds are very low that you're going to suddenly and surprisingly grow like a rocket ship. Just know that if you end up needing to ask for an extension to the maturity date, the investor is going to want to put a cap in place to protect them.

SUMMARIZING STARTUP SUCCESS

The various stages of funding can be fulfilled with a variety of funding sources, each with a corresponding legal investment instrument. The factors that make for a logical and ideal combination of source and instrument include the stage of the company, the amount to be raised, and the personal goals and preferences of the company executives. For technology startups in the pre-seed or seed stage, convertible securities are the most popular instrument when raising small amounts ($1 million or less) from friends and family or angel investors. They are also popular for bridge rounds between almost any consecutive stages.

A key reason convertible securities are so popular for these situations is their extreme level of flexibility and ease of use. Technically speaking, each investor in a given round of funding could be presented a convertible security with different terms. That is certainly not advisable because of the administrative nightmare and likely perception of unfairness among the investors, should they find out; but it does attest to the extreme level of flexibility that is offered. In fact, even the concept of a *funding round* is not nearly as rigid when convertible securities are used. The rolling close nature of funding rounds that utilize convertible securities means that with each closed investor, new cash hits the bank account and can immediately be put to use. This hand-to-mouth aspect of the rolling close can also be distracting and disjointing if a funding round stretches out over a long period of time. That's because the company can't really shift a gear like intended, but rather has to take incremental steps along the way, just in case the full target amount isn't reached.

The ease-of-use aspect of convertible securities translates to lower legal costs. Once a term sheet and funding document are papered up by your corporate attorney, you will be able to make any needed tweaks for specific investors and do most of the work with minimal involvement from your attorney.

Although a convertible security is both flexible and easy to use, that doesn't mean the various terms that need to be set are simple or unimportant. The terms really matter and must be set with care. For example, as was described, setting the valuation cap way too low could have serious negative implications to your future equity round of funding. But used effectively, a convertible security with the right terms will enable you to close your funding round as quickly as possible so that you can get off the fundraising trail and get your head 100% back into growing a great business.

AHA MOMENTS

1. Convertible securities allow an investor's investment to convert to equity in the future once their more desired preferred class of stock is available.

2. The discount and valuation cap serve as the investor's primary economic benefit versus the valuation offered to the future equity investors.

3. The valuation cap is not intended to set an exact valuation for the company at the time the funding is raised. Instead, it is intended to serve as a protection mechanism for the investor in the event the company grows more aggressively than expected and is able to earn a valuation that is considerably higher than expected. However, investors will comprehend the possibility of converting to equity using the cap amount, which means it must be perceived as *reasonable*.

4. For future equity conversion, the holder of a convertible security gets either the discounted valuation or the valuation cap amount, whichever is more favorable to them.

5. The SAFE is not considered a debt instrument like a convertible note is. As a result, it does not have a maturity date (term) or interest rate. The lack of a maturity date might cause an investor to consider it less investor friendly, because there is no forcing function in the future for converting to equity or paying back their investment.

6. If using a SAFE, decide whether you want to use the original version with a pre-money valuation cap or the newer post-money version. The conversion mechanics are different.

7. Since a convertible note is considered a debt instrument, investors might stand in a more favorable payback priority position if the company is liquidated or sold in distress.

8. When convertible securities are used to support a bridge round, the term is usually short, and the discount is often lower than when used for a traditional round of funding.

CHAPTER 6

THE SEED
FUNDRAISING DANCE

"Whether you think you can or think you can't, you're right."

—Henry Ford

L ike fundraising campaigns in general, the part when you're
spending 80% of all your time actually pitching investors for investment can also be further broken into start,
middle, and end phases. And for seed funding campaigns that
utilize convertible securities, there is a fairly definable rhythm
throughout these phases. This is because of the *rolling close* phenomenon. There often isn't a traditional lead investor that invests
half or more of the target funding amount. Instead, a dozen or
more angel investors each typically invest $25,000 to $50,000 on

independent timelines. There is no coordinated closing event for the whole funding round.

It is possible to raise a seed round from institutional investors or a combination of institutional and angel investors. But those seed rounds are typically larger in size ($1.5 million or larger) and are usually equity rounds of funding in which preferred stock is sold. Because of all this, they have a rhythm that is more similar to a Series A round of funding.

The rolling close that is possible by using convertible securities introduces some opportunities and some burdens. It is nice to be able to get a check from an angel, deposit it in the company bank account, and immediately put it to use. But a rolling close also introduces the risk of closing some angel investors in the starting phase only to later discover that the terms aren't attractive enough to fill out the rest of the funding round. And without an institutional investor to invest half or more of the total target funding amount, the risk profile for angel investors during the rolling close changes quite dramatically throughout the fund raising campaign phases.

START: SECURING THE FIRST INVESTORS

For funding rounds that utilize convertible securities, the first 20% or so is by far the hardest to close. Think about it from the investor's perspective. If you have a target to raise $1 million and they write the first $25,000 check, what happens if you aren't successful raising any more funding? Their investment is basically dead on arrival. So instead, if they like the investment opportunity, they will want to write the last $25,000 check after you've already reached $975,000. The first investments in the funding round are the riskiest, and conversely, the last investments are the least risky. Angel investing is already recognized as a very risky activity, so just avoiding the starting phase of a funding round can be an important part of an investor's strategy.

Investors you pitch during the starting phase won't usually come right out and tell you they don't want to be the first investor. Instead, they will give you another homework assignment, ask for another meeting to dive into a different part of your business, or otherwise find ways to drag things out in hopes that you will raise some money from other investors first. But if no investor is willing to write the first check, how can you ever get your seed round closed?

I'll give an analogy. If you have ever been to a wedding, you probably have observed this phenomenon. After a beautiful ceremony and fabulous dinner, the reception party starts. The DJ plays some great, upbeat dance songs, but the dance floor is empty. After a few songs, the groom's Aunt Sally and Uncle Fred get just drunk enough to jump onto the dance floor. Immediately, 10 other couples follow suit, and the dance floor is hoppin'. If you don't already have investors beating on your door to invest in your seed round, your mission during the starting phase is to get some investor on the dance floor so that others will follow suit.

FAVORABLE TERMS

If the very first investors in the round are taking more risk, should they get the exact same terms as the last investors in the same round? The flexible nature of convertible securities allows you to vary the terms, as necessary, for situations like this. Consider offering more favorable economics to the first investors by presenting them with different terms.

The favorable terms can be aligned with the first 10% to 20% of the target amount for the round. For example, if you're raising $1 million in total, the first $100,000 to $200,000 worth of investment would come with more favorable terms.

With convertible securities, the most logical terms to modify are the valuation cap, the discount, or both. You can offer a lower valuation cap (i.e., $4.5 million instead of $5 million) or a higher discount (i.e., 25% instead of 20%). The adjustment often doesn't need to be significant, but rather just enough to catch the early investors' attention and to demonstrate that you understand they will be taking on additional risk if they invest first.

There are two ways of communicating these favorable terms for the first investors. You can come right out and mention it in your term sheet. With this, you would show the standard terms while also messaging the favorable terms that are being offered to the first batch of investment. Alternatively, you could decide to only make verbal mention of the favorable terms during your interaction with investors. I have seen both approaches work favorably, and I mostly recommend the verbal approach to startups that aren't quite sure if the favorable terms will be needed to secure the first investors. There's no reason to offer the favorable terms if they aren't needed to get your funding round kick-started. And you can always start with the verbal approach and later modify the term sheet if you want to be more formal about the special offer.

VERBAL COMMITMENTS

A second tool for getting some first checks written is verbal commitments. You can use this either instead of or in addition to favorable terms. You basically ask the first highly interested investors to initially commit only verbally. In other words, if they seem to have decided to make an investment but aren't reaching for their checkbook, let them know you understand that you're still very early in your fundraising cycle and ask if you can consider them verbally committed. If they are agreeable, ask what they will need to see before they will write their check. Most likely it's raising a certain amount from others first. Perhaps you only need to reach 10% of the total target amount. It is really important to understand what bar you need to reach to secure their follow-through. If they like the idea of investing alongside other first investors but won't give a full verbal commitment as such, there are other issues at hand that you will need to uncover. Do so by asking the following question: "Beyond my reaching (a specified amount) in closed funding, what else is it that you would need to see in order for this to be an exciting investment opportunity for you?" Then have your paper and pen handy.

You want to use your first verbal commit to help secure your second one, and so forth until you've reached the bar to have a virtual check-writing party. For this, you are best served if you are able to mention both the committed investor's name and the committed amount. So before leaving the meeting, ask their permission. If they agree, and depending on how positive their vibe is, you could also ask if they would be willing to exchange an email with you to that effect so that you can further use it as a tool to secure the next investments. Some angel investors will do this, but many won't, so ask diplomatically.

Now it's time for the check-writing party, but you don't need to get all of the investors together in the same room. Instead, once you've achieved the goal for closing out the first committed investors, get them each to sign the investment documents. Once that's done, let them each know it has been done, and ask them to transfer the money.

You might discover that you have to continue using tools like favorable terms and verbal commits until you've reached 25% or more of your target amount. But regardless, once you get to about 30% of the target, the starting phase of closing investors is done, and the dynamics will start to change.

MIDDLE: THE GRIND

After closing the first part of your funding round, there's no way to best describe the next phase other than a true grind. Your mission during this middle phase is to reach a genuine downhill slope for your round. I'm talking about something in the range of 65% of your total target. Whereas the starting phase involves selectively finding the first-movers, this phase involves tons of meetings and often tons of disappointment along the way to that 65%.

By now, your prioritized target investor list should be robust, and with the first investors closed, you should know who to go after next. In fact, there should be some investors that have given clear indications of interest but specifically rejected your attempts to close them using favorable terms or verbal commits. Now that you've got the first chunk of your round closed and with money in the bank, those are the best investors to approach again.

Keeping *all* interested but not-yet-committed investors warm is critical to generating and maintaining the needed momentum in and through this middle phase. You can best do this by including them on your monthly emailed company updates. This way, when you approach them again more formally, they should already know how you've progressed since the last discussion, including some status of your active funding round. The monthly updates are extra work and maybe even a pain in the ass. Too bad. If you don't send them like clockwork, your previously interested investors will go cold, and you will have taken two big steps backwards with each of them.

Your most significant assets for this middle phase are pure hard work and a positive attitude. But there are a couple of other tools to use. One is a system for tracking and managing your investor interactions. Grouping investors in ways that make the most sense to you (possibly by your assessment of their odds of investing), capturing information you want to remember about your conversations, and recording logical next steps are all important to reduce the chaos. Most fundraisers just use a spreadsheet, but with select color-coded text and highlights to visually assist with the sheer volume of information.

The second tool to use is specific messaging to convey the progress of your funding round. By now, you have a combination of new money in the bank from checks written, signed documents still waiting on funding, and verbal commitments. If those amounts, respectively, for a $1 million funding round are $250,000, $100,000, and $50,000, how would you answer the following question: "So how much have you raised so far?" Your answer could be anywhere between $250,000 and $400,000, depending on the definition of *raised so far*. I think it's totally acceptable to respond with $400,000 if you make it clear that it includes commitments: "Including recent commits, we've already raised $400,000." I don't know about you, but to me, that sounds like you're almost at the halfway mark and certainly better than just at the 25% mark ($250,000 cash in hand). Just make sure the commitments are legitimate and referenceable, because any investor is going to want to know the exact breakdown of in-the-bank, signed, and verbal commits.

The final tool to continue using when you can't seem to figure out why a particular investor won't give their commitment is the magic question: "What is it that you would need to see in order for this to be an exciting investment for you?" Variations of this exact question help create an environment whereby the investor can't easily ask for another meeting or issue another homework assignment just because they either can't make a decision or already know they won't invest but simply don't want to tell you. To either of those, you can reply, "Sounds good. So in addition to bringing (insert homework assignment) to review during our next meeting, is there anything else you will need to see in order for this to be an exciting investment for you?" Grind, grind, grind until you get to 65% of your fundraising target.

You should assume that every investor has attention deficit disorder (ADD), whether it's true or not. Active investors see lots of deals, and yours is just one of them. If they seem really excited by the end of your meeting, that's great. But that excitement has an extremely short shelf life. It wears off unbelievably fast, and that's partly because of the other exciting investment opportunities they come across after your meeting. You must find excuses to get back in front of them, either in person or otherwise. Your monthly stakeholder updates will help with this, and so will follow-through on any homework assignments they gave you. Sharing progress on traction is always the best way to remain top of mind with investors suffering from ADD.

END: CLOSING OUT THE ROUND

The hardest part is now behind you for sure. That doesn't mean finishing the final 35% of your target will be easy; it just won't be as chaotic. You are now ready to close the most conservative of the interested investors—the ones that truly want to be the last check written—or close to it. You might also find that brand-new investors you encounter move quickly through their decision process because they realize you're close to the end.

As you enter this phase, your messaging about fundraising progress should absolutely change. Whereas previously you mentioned how much of your target amount you have *closed*, now you want to message the *scarcity*. For example, "We're raising $1 million and only have $150,000 left. Can I save you a slot?" What, you mean there might not be a slot left to invest if the investor doesn't move quickly? Absolutely, that's what you want them to conclude. If you truly have the fundraising momentum as you enter this final phase, this will play out extremely well to your advantage. If, instead, you barely limped into this final phase, you probably won't get the desired reaction. But in either case, you should message the small amount left that will enable you to achieve global world domination and make the investor a ton of money in return.

Since getting to the 65% mark that puts you on the downhill slope is so significant, you will also want to think about how you message the overall target size for your round. When you previously determined the right amount to raise, you might have explored different scenarios with different sets of future outcomes. Let's say those two amounts were $1 million as a baseline scenario and $1.35 million for something a little more exciting. Reaching the downhill slope for each equates to $650,000 and $877,500, respectively. This means that if you message that you are raising $1 million and have an oversubscription allowance up to $1.35 million, you can start using "we only have (insert specific amount) left" messaging starting at $650,000 rather than having to climb to $877,500. But in order to execute this messaging successfully, the $1 million baseline scenario must still yield a set of future outcomes that investors can get excited about.

GETTING STUCK

It is possible to get stuck at any point toward your ultimate target. Because of this, *do not* increase spending based on your total fundraising target once investments start coming in or even after reaching 65% of the target and entering the downhill slope. Instead, with each increment of new funding raised (in the bank, not verbally committed), only increase your spending with the assumption that you will not raise any additional funding. I regularly see startups get ahead of their skis by increasing their spending beyond the real investments they've received. Unwinding those commitments often means personnel layoffs, which are painful, embarrassing, and unsettling for the remaining team.

There is a common rolling close scenario that causes the most frustration and confusion about how to best proceed with your campaign. It relates to getting through the middle phase and not having enough of a pipeline of interested investors to fully close out the round. The scenario I see most often is getting stuck somewhere in the range of 75% of the original target. The reason it's such a dilemma is that the ultimate goal is within sight, the effort required to get to 75% was significant, and forfeiting the missing 25% of funding changes the expected outcomes enough to make a meaningful difference. Founders find themselves not wanting to give up. That is admirable but may not be the best decision.

If you find yourself in this situation, you might be inclined to dial your fundraising efforts back to 30% of your time so that energy can be put back into the business. After all, your co-founders and coworkers have been picking up your slack since you dialed up to 80%. But in truth, the best approach is to first step back and closely assess the situation to decide whether you should remain at 80% of your time or stop fundraising altogether. Anything in between is going to result in huge disappointment. Dialing down to 30% or even 40% of your time will not allow you to close out the remaining funding, yet it will still put your business results in some jeopardy. It's a lose-lose situation.

Remember that the rolling close nature of using convertible securities means that you can officially pause fundraising but later come across an ideal investor that is able to make a quick decision. If minimal effort can close them as an investor, you can make a one-off decision without officially resuming your campaign. Think of it like a small but unexpected shot in the arm.

As for assessing your situation, there are a few things to scrutinize very carefully. After doing so, it will hopefully be clear whether it's best to remain fully engaged or to pause the fundraising efforts. I say *pause* rather than *stop* because certain conditions could exist in the near future that cause you to resume your efforts, and the flexible nature of using convertible securities is very supportive of that situation.

INVESTOR PIPELINE

If your investor pipeline has run completely dry or if only poor-quality investor prospects remain, your answer is clear. Pause fundraising because spinning up fresh investor prospects is going to take too long and too much energy. One exception would be if you've been invited to a demo-day pitching event with a meaningful prize for the winner and a good theme for what you're working on. Another is if you have been selected to pitch an angel network with a track record of investing in startups like yours. In these two cases, minimal time and effort could yield a worthwhile outcome.

COMMON INVESTOR CONCERNS

For the investors that decided not to invest, what were their reasons? Among the reasons, are there any common themes or issues? If so, can you solve those issues in the near term? Being able to easily or quickly solve a small number of issues that, after doing so, will *reliably* unlock additional investment might be enough justification to continue the campaign. Otherwise, pause where you are and put your energy back into the business.

NEED FOR THE REMAINING ADDITIONAL CAPITAL

Time has gone by since the fundraising campaign started, which means you should be a lot smarter about your business venture. Some of the assumptions you were making for your business plan might now be validated, and some of your original financial projections might have been too conservative. In other words, you might not absolutely require the full original fundraising target in order to achieve enough outcomes to successfully raise your next round of funding. Of course, the opposite could be true, which leaves you even more desperate to close the remaining funding.

SPLITTING THE FUNDING ROUND

You don't want to create a scenario in which you are staring directly at the fundraising chasm. But that most often happens when the company has progressed enough to be out of the sweet spot for seed-stage investors and not yet in the sweet spot for Series A investors. If you have already raised enough capital to gain sufficient additional traction and other accomplishments, while still matching the investment criteria for seed-stage investors, you can formally split your seed funding stage into two rounds: seed 1 and seed 2. The newly revised purpose of your current seed 1 is to achieve a step-up in valuation for seed 2, whose purpose will be to get you to the Series A sweet spot.

If you're already implementing this strategy and it's your seed 1 that is stuck at 75% of the target, you might not get a step-up in valuation for seed 2. And if it's your seed 2 that is stuck at 75%, you will need to raise a bridge round to get to the Series A sweet spot. Like I said before, there are numerous evolutionary paths and associated fundraising strategies for startups.

SUMMARIZING STARTUP SUCCESS

I often use the analogy of toppling dominos to describe securing the first investors for a new round of funding. After toppling the first domino, the others follow, assuming the arrangement is specifically planned out. Spacing is critical, and navigating around curves, creative structures, or fancy elevations gets tricky and takes even more careful planning. When a funding round goes exactly as planned, it has a certain cadence that starts with the first investors making commitments (the first domino), and that, in turn, gives the momentum to secure the majority of the rest of the investors (dominos toppling other dominos). That, in turn, helps secure the final investors (the grand finale of the domino-toppling performance). Figure 6.1 gives a visual summary of what a seed fundraising dance might entail along the way to reaching 100% of the target funding amount.

Finding interested investors, meeting with them multiple times,

digesting their objections and concerns, fielding numerous homework assignments, and trying to learn from—but not get demoral-
ized by—outright rejections involves an absolute grind that is hard
to describe. But it is something you should expect so as to not be
totally disillusioned going into the process. Just the sheer number
of meetings required to close a typical round of funding is daunt-
ing. That's why you have no choice but to spend 80% or more of
your time on fundraising once the formal campaign begins and
until it either naturally comes to a conclusion (reaches the target)
or you choose to bring it to a conclusion.

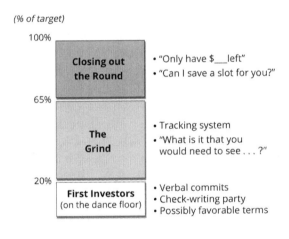

Figure 6.1. The dance of the rolling close

If you hit a wall at any point along the way, you've got to step
back and do some serious evaluation and soul-searching to determine what's going on and what to do next. This is why the strategy
and planning phases of fundraising are so important. They reduce
the odds of hitting the wall, and, in many cases, they at least push

the wall further towards your desired target amount. You would much rather hit the wall at 85% of your target than 35%. Regardless of hitting a wall, if your vision and business potential are still legitimately valid, keep making forward progress using whatever means are necessary. If no more funding is available at the time, get creative about advancing your business using other means—of course, within ethical and legal boundaries. The best entrepreneurs I work with are amazing, creative survivalists. Your time spent earlier as a bootstrapper will pay dividends in this scenario.

This chapter was about seed rounds of funding. What about Series A rounds—are they the same? Well, as you will soon learn, there are definitely some similarities. But there are also some unique differences that are very important to understand.

 ## AHA MOMENTS

1. Seed rounds that use convertible securities allow for a rolling close, which means you get to put each new investor's money to work as soon as they sign the docs and write you a check.

2. Seed rounds that are led by an institutional investor and involve selling equity have a rhythm that is more like a Series A.

3. With a rolling close, the risk profile changes dramatically throughout the progressive closing of the round, with the earliest investments being the riskiest. Because of this, special economic incentives might be needed to close the first investors and gain the needed initial momentum.

4. Verbal commitments can serve as a good tool to close a collection of first investors together so that none is technically the first investor.

5. Verbal commitments are often included when messaging how much of the round has been closed, but make sure they are truly committed, and be prepared to provide details about the breakdown of verbal commitments versus fully closed investments. Exaggerating will cause credibility issues, and outright lying will be a disqualification.

6. Once on the downhill slope of the round (at 65% or more of the total target), start messaging the scarcity factor of how much is still available rather than how much has been closed.

7. Upon hitting a wall, dialing down from 80% is not the best option. Instead, objectively assess the situation, and decide whether to continue at that pace, pause the campaign until conditions improve, or officially terminate the round.

CHAPTER 7

SERIES A FUNDRAISING

"You miss 100% of the shots you never take."

—Wayne Gretzky, hockey Hall of Famer

Series A is an equity round of funding and, as such, doesn't allow for a rolling close like with convertible securities. Instead, you have to first secure a formal *lead investor* by agreeing on a set of terms that all other investors in the round will also use as they invest. These terms are initially memorialized using a term sheet. Sometimes, verbal negotiations precede the creation of a term sheet, and other times, the interested lead investor uses a term sheet as the vehicle to present their initial investment offer.

DEFINITION: TERM SHEET

A term sheet outlines the key and material terms of your funding activity. For a seed round of funding using a convertible security, the company often conveys a high-level summary of their proposed terms via a term sheet. It is shared with interested investors first, before the full legal document is sent for execution.

For an equity round of funding, the term sheet is instead produced by interested lead investors and used to communicate their proposed offer. It usually fits on a few pages and is the key instrument during the negotiation phase of the funding round. Once the terms are agreed on and the term sheet is executed, it serves as guidance for the attorneys as they produce the full set of legal execution documents to close the round of funding.

The lead investor for a Series A is most likely an institutional investor, such as a venture fund. They typically invest one-third or more of the target investment total for the round. This means the remainder needs to be secured after the term sheet is signed, and the lead investor often assists with that effort. It is rare that the lead investor consumes the whole round, but it can happen.

Unless they're going to invest the full amount needed for the round, Series A lead investors protect themselves by setting a required minimum amount to close the round. If you don't secure enough additional investment to reach that amount, you don't get any of the investors' money. This means the more of the round the lead investor takes for themselves and the more realistic the required closing total is, the higher the odds are of achieving a successful close.

The lack of a rolling close causes the Series A dance to be a little different than what was described for a seed round using convertible securities. Rather than three defined phases for closing investors, there are usually only two. The first phase focuses on securing the lead investor with a signed term sheet, and the second phase focuses on securing the remaining investors needed to close the round. A third phase might be necessary due to what's called an *oversubscription allowance* (more on that later in the chapter).

GETTING TO THE TERM SHEET

Not all venture funds will serve as lead investors. This means that, during the planning phase of your Series A campaign, you need to determine which venture funds will lead versus which will only follow (invest after a term sheet is secured). Some will do both.

The lead investor doesn't just negotiate the investment terms and write the largest check for the round; they also usually take a more active role with the company. A good example is taking one or more of the board of directors seats, which gives them some oversight and governance responsibilities but also calls for them to be strategic advisors of sorts. Not all venture funds are equipped to be that active, which might be a reason they only follow rather than lead rounds.

The objective of this first phase of a Series A campaign is to secure a term sheet with favorable, or at least reasonable, terms. This means prioritizing investors that can serve as the lead. In a perfect world, multiple prospective leads will move at the same pace of evaluation, and several will also decide to present a term sheet for your consideration. With this scenario, you are in the best position to negotiate an optimal set of terms with the lead investor you feel will best serve your interests. Unfortunately, it rarely plays out that way. But if you don't orchestrate your meetings and try to nudge slow-moving investors to the next step, you could be presented with a single term sheet and have no other alternatives. It would be similar to interviewing for a job with a single company rather than several.

There is clearly a benefit to executing a process that gives you the best chance of receiving multiple term sheets in a similar time frame. Evaluating investors during the relationship-building phase and then prioritizing them accordingly is the first step to achieving this. Then, as you officially pitch them for investment, you should gauge where you are in *their* process for making an investment decision. They only issue term sheets after deciding they want to serve as the lead investor. At the end of a meeting with them, ask what the next steps are and how you can best support their process. You're trying to figure out two things: Are they truly interested? How long will their evaluation process take?

If you're dealing with an analyst, associate, or principal within the firm, you're still in the early or middle phase of their evaluation. Once your investment opportunity gets picked up by a partner or, better yet, a general partner (GP), you're getting close to a real decision. This means that spending excessive time and energy with an analyst or associate can be a waste. At some point, you've got to find a way to engage with a partner or GP. If you get a request to pitch at the weekly GP meeting, the next step will either be a decision (yes or no) or a request for more information.

There is a significant benefit to knowing where you stand with multiple prospective lead investors on their respective paths to a decision. It allows you to determine where extra energy should be applied to get them all lined up with each other. Again, this is way easier said than done but worth an attempt. Even just getting two term sheets in a similar time frame is hugely favorable to a solo offer.

SHARING INFORMATION

The prospective lead investor will require a decent amount of information to support their evaluation. But you should realize they will also enjoy an exclusive period of due diligence after the term sheet is signed. This enables them to double-confirm some assumptions and also to get into more granular details. I mention this because leading up to the term sheet, you should only be expected to provide information that's needed to help the investor decide if they want to invest and, if so, what their proposed key terms will be. For example, they surely need historical financial results at a high level and information about any significant customers, but they don't need a detailed list of every customer going back to the beginning of time. They rightfully deserve to see a summary version of your cap table with details on key equity holders; but they don't need all of the board consents that authorized the granting of the equity. They need to understand your product roadmap; but they don't get to do a source code review. You get the idea.

Investors might ask for far more information than needed to present a term sheet, and it's up to you to decide whether and when to diplomatically push back. One way to head this off is to create an online shared repository referred to as a *data room*. In this data room, you will put all of the basic information you predict most lead investors will need. Using a data room hints at what you're initially willing to share and also minimizes the chaos of servicing multiple requests for different types of information—just grant them access to the data room. If an investor requests something extra and you agree it's useful and appropriate, give it to them and then decide whether the other investors would benefit from having it in the data room.

DATA ROOM:
PRE-TERM-SHEET DUE DILIGENCE

Before an investor will offer a term sheet, they'll need certain information. The following items may be the most useful in your data room:

- Current pitch deck

- Certificate and articles of incorporation, including any amendments

- Summary version of pre-investment capitalization table (include line-item detail for any founders, key executives, and significant investors)

- Financial statements (P&L, balance sheet) covering at least the prior four quarters

- Financial projections—at least 24 months

- Bylaws, including any amendments

- Prior rounds of funding, including the total amount raised and key terms for each

- Summaries of any patent or trademark filings

THE SHAPE OF THE CURVE MATTERS

During the seed stage, you don't have enough of a track record to create fancy graphs over long periods of time. But that's not the case leading into a Series A, when you should have lots of metrics that can be trended over time to tell a story. Series A investors want to evaluate each of these trended metrics to help gain insights into your historical track record and to compare that to the stories they hear from you.

I often get asked how much revenue is needed to successfully raise a Series A. I can tell the entrepreneur wants me to confirm what they might have read in various articles or heard from their advisors. A very simplistic answer might be something like $1.5 million in annualized revenue. But, like many things in the world of a startup, the right answer is far from that simple.

Series A investors evaluating a startup selling a mobile app with viral adoption or a medical device requiring FDA approval might not expect any revenue at all. But if they come across one selling enterprise hardware or software, they might be looking for $1.5 million or more. There is no broadly applicable revenue target to strive for. And even my mention of $1.5 million could be considerably high or low compared to the expectation for your business. Interactions with prospective Series A investors well before you plan to launch the fundraising campaign are the only way to identify your ideal revenue target.

THE SLOPE OF THE CURVE

The slope of the curve for a given trended metric is very telling. To visualize this point, check out the three scenarios in figure 7.1. The Fast company reaches only $1.0 million in revenue but does so in 12 months, while the Slow company reaches a seemingly more impressive $1.5 million, but it takes 24 months to do so. The Fast company might have more success fundraising, even though their revenue is lower than the Slow company's. Just imagine where the Fast company will be after another 6–12 months.

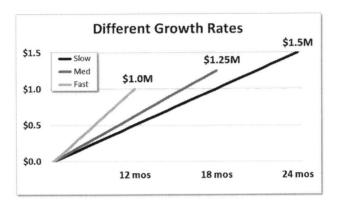

Figure 7.1. Three hypothetical growth trajectories

There is actually nothing wrong with the Slow company. Their growth rate in absolute terms isn't actually slow at all, but rather just a lot slower than the Fast company's rate. In fact, if only the Slow company were shown on the graphic, we would all probably be impressed. But venture capitalists (VCs) see a lot of investment opportunities, which means they are going to come across all three types of companies shown on the graph, and they will make the comparison before deciding where to deploy their capital. And although I used a revenue metric for the prior examples, I want to reiterate that Series A investors make evaluations using trended results for a variety of key business metrics.

ACCELERATION VERSUS DECELERATION

The graphs in the figure above are too perfectly linear. No company grows at the exact same rate month over month for long periods of time. A typical company's revenue results don't form a line but rather a curve. The shape of that curve really matters.

Take note of the two startups represented in figure 7.2. They both start at around $900,000, and both reach $1.5 million over a six-month period. But hopefully you notice a dramatic difference between the two companies. Which is a VC going to be more excited about? Clearly, the startup that is gaining momentum (acceleration of growth) is more exciting. Imagine what the next six months for each of these companies is probably going to look like. If your own graphs suggest you are losing momentum for a key metric, many VCs will delay their decision to see what happens.

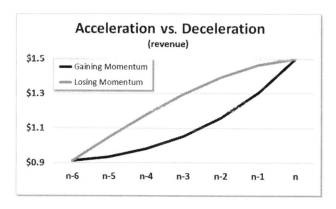

Figure 7.2. Revenue acceleration and deceleration

Figure 7.2 plots the companies' actual revenue, whereas figure 7.3 plots the growth *rate* from period to period. Notice how even more obvious the difference is with figure 7.3. What might have happened to the company that is losing momentum? Perhaps they overinvested in the early days to gain traction, only to later discover their customer acquisition strategy wasn't efficient. Maybe they hit a rough spot, had to do a layoff, and then started to wobble. There are numerous scenarios that could cause either of the curves to happen, and the investors want to know the underlying story. Again, the shape of the curve for various trended metrics really matters to your fundraising success. What stories do the slopes of your curves suggest to the investor?

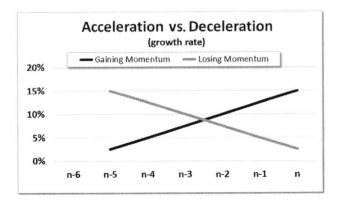

Figure 7.3. Growth-rate acceleration and deceleration

ADDITIONAL SCENARIOS

Even the above graph shows growth curves that are too smooth versus what's likely to be experienced by a given startup. In figure 7.4, you will see some scenarios I commonly observe for the very limited percentage of startups that reach really interesting revenue milestones like $100 million. The titles next to each curve suggest a possible story behind the numbers.

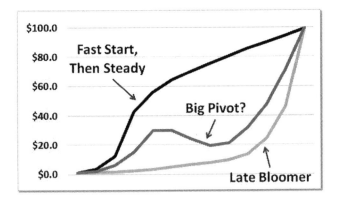

Figure 7.4. Various growth trajectories

GETTING TO $100 MILLION

You won't be anywhere close to $100 million in revenues when you raise your Series A, but a discussion about what it will take to get there certainly could be on the investor's mind. It is both a big and round number, and it could lead to an acquisition that gets the investor a suitable return on their investment.

What if I told you that you had 10 years to reach $100 million? That's PLENTY of time, right? Ten years seems like a really long time, and we all know examples of tech startups reaching that figure in considerably less than 10 years. So why couldn't that be you? It absolutely could, but it's much more amazingly difficult than most people think.

Figure 7.5 is a hypothetical year-by-year path to $100 million, including the associated annual growth rates. Notice that although the company's yearly revenues increase over the entire period, the growth rate—the percentage increase of those revenues—slows considerably.

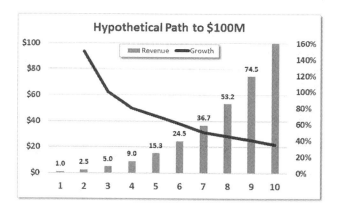

Figure 7.5. Growing to $100 million

The early years in this scenario, where growth rates are 100% or more, certainly can happen, especially since the company is starting from a relatively small base. But continuing to deliver 50% to 70% growth rates in the middle years and even sustaining 35% to 45% growth in the last couple of years is so amazingly difficult that it's hard for me to describe. If you experience a pivot or two during the early years, like most startups do, your revenue might flatten or even decline during that same period. I see a lot of startups that take three years or more just to reach their first $1 million and then get a flywheel going for solid growth.

I've been a part of three reasonably aggressive growth scenarios during my 29-year professional career. In figure 7.6 below, I've listed the annual revenue results from the time I joined until our exit. I can tell you with honesty that each of the rocket ships were vibrating as if they were about to explode during most of the journeys. Just imagine what it is like inside a company that reaches $50 million or more in a few short years after being founded.

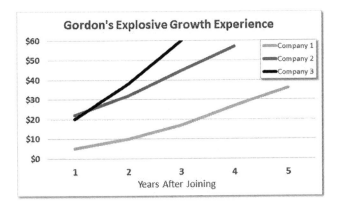

Figure 7.6. Gordon's growth experiences

TERM SHEETS ARE PERISHABLE

A presented term sheet for investment doesn't remain open for acceptance forever. In fact, they are often only valid for two to three days. If that's not restrictive enough, they also come with what's referred to as a *no shop* clause. That's basically a confidentiality requirement that disallows you from letting other prospective lead investors know about the terms you've agreed to after signing the term sheet. And although a signed term sheet itself is nonbinding, that just means the investor isn't yet legally required to invest. But it also means you can't continue soliciting other lead investors for a better offer. The lead investor basically wants—and deserves—an uninterrupted period of 30 to 60 days in which to complete their due diligence and finalize the investment documents.

Since you probably won't have all of the prospective lead investors lined up to present you with term sheets in the same 48 to 72-hour period, you will need to be tactical once the first term sheet is presented. There are two techniques to use in tandem. First, let any other prospective lead investors know you've received a term sheet but haven't yet signed it. They will want to know who the investor is, what the authorized amount of the round is, and what the key terms are. I recommend that you only let them know the authorized amount. Keep the rest confidential, and let the other investors know that, although you and your attorney are still evaluating the details, you wanted them to know about the term sheet, since you will only have a couple of days to make a decision. It's amazing how fast interested investors will move following such a notice, even if it means giving you an answer you don't want.

In parallel, try to buy yourself more time with the investor who presented the term sheet. Engage in a back-and-forth dialogue about the terms. Seek clarification, and start some negotiation on items that don't seem fair or that aren't to your liking. This process alone should add days to the process and possibly more. Just be careful not to stretch it out so far that they rescind their offer. They know exactly what you are doing and will want to move quickly through these negotiations. That's only fair.

There are numerous terms included on a term sheet. Some have more significant impact than others, and you should seek a set of terms that is both balanced and fair. Because of this, the negotiation process usually involves making trade-offs based on what's most important to each party. We won't address the specific terms or how to negotiate them here, but Brad Feld and Jason Mendelson's book *Venture Deals* is an excellent resource for those topics.

FROM TERM SHEET TO CLOSE

After the term sheet is signed, two things will happen in parallel. The lead investor will proceed with deeper due diligence, and lawyers from both sides will get to work on the legal documents needed to close the round. At the same time, you and your new lead investor will seek other investors to fill out the rest of the round. This phase of the process looks much like the final phase of a seed round using convertible securities. In other words, you're hopefully already on the downhill slope—or close—because of the lead investor's committed amount. This means you can start messaging the scarcity (i.e., "We are raising $7.5 million and only have $2 million left").

You want to work closely with your lead investor on this phase for a couple of reasons. First, they likely have suggestions for improving your pitch deck and messaging. Second, you don't want to accidentally go after the same investors that your lead investor will reach out to. This just takes some basic coordination. But you absolutely should expect your new lead investor to help you close out the round and conduct weekly check-ins with them, at a minimum. As commitments come in, you and your lead investor will tally how much more is needed to reach the required amount to close.

DATA ROOM:
POST-TERM-SHEET DUE DILIGENCE

The following items will be crucial for your investors once you have a signed term sheet. However, some of this information may be requested before a term sheet is in place, so be ready for that possibility.

- Term sheet and funding execution documents

- All documented board actions and meeting minutes

- All documented stockholder actions

- A corporate structure chart and a list of all subsidiaries

- A detailed version of your capitalization table

- All historical stock price fair market values for each class of stock

- A list of your current employees and independent contractors, including their roles, current compensation, and any deferred compensation

- Any employment agreements with company founders and executives

- Signed intellectual property assignment forms and license agreements

- All equity incentive and employee stock plans

- Expected new post-funding hires, including proposed job titles, hiring timeline, and expected compensation

continued

- Descriptions of any open or settled legal actions, lawsuits, cease-and-desist notices, employee harassment claims, or similar workplace-related claims in which the company is named as a party
- Descriptions of any side letters granting special rights to investors or service providers
- The company's privacy policy, terms of service agreement, or similar documents governing customer use of the company's product
- Regulatory and compliance standards the company currently adheres to and whether an independent audit has been completed
- The company's business insurance policies

OVERSUBSCRIPTION

Some term sheets have two milestones for closing the round. Once you reach the *initial close* or *first close* funding target, you are able to go through a legal closing process and get your hands on that amount of new capital to put to work. The new investors will then be on your cap table, and the new preferred shareholder rights will take effect.

The other close is called a *second close* or *final close* and is put in place to allow for the possibility of excess investor interest and what's referred to as *oversubscription*. This doesn't exactly add a true rolling close attribute to your round, but it does give you the possibility of taking on more funding than you absolutely require. Additionally, it gives you extra time to close the oversubscription amounts. For example, the term sheet might call for $7.5 million to qualify for an initial close, and you might be required to reach that milestone within 60 days of signing the term sheet. You might further be given an additional 45 days in which to raise up to $1.5 million of oversubscription to be secured during the final close. If, within the initial 60-day period, you reach $8 million, you can complete an initial close and get your hands on that amount. But you then only have up to $1 million allowed for oversubscription.

CORPORATE VENTURE CAPITAL

Not all venture funds are alike, but corporate venture capital (CVC) is different enough from the rest to justify an explanation. Some corporations invest in early-stage ventures for a variety of reasons. Some do it because of the potential synergies with their own business. Investing in early-stage innovation helps them keep a close eye on future trends and could also lead to strategic partnerships or acquisitions. Because of this, they are often referred to as *strategics* rather than VCs or venture funds. Other corporations invest more for a return on their investment, similar to traditional venture funds.

If you find yourself with corporate venture prospects, first find out their motivations for making investments in early-stage companies. If they are investing solely for business synergies, you might discover that the investments are made directly off their balance sheet, and not in seed or Series A rounds of funding but rather Series B and later growth rounds with companies that can deliver more of an immediate impact to their results. With this, they are often less sensitive to valuation and other terms and more sensitive to business synergies. If, instead, they set up a separate legal entity for making investments, then they are optimizing for some combination of return on investment (ROI), like a traditional venture fund, and business synergies. Your mission is to find out the relative importance of each to determine how well your opportunity is aligned.

To make this determination, first check to see if they have a separate website for an entity that includes the name of their company plus the word *ventures* in the title. If one exists, do they have investment professionals with titles like *general partner* or *managing director*? These are indicators of operating like a more traditional venture fund. Next, review their portfolio of investments via either their website or SEC filings to determine how many of their portfolio companies have direct synergies with their core business. Finally, during one of your first meetings with them, ask questions to confirm your suspicions about their motivations and strategies for making strategic investments. They won't be shy about providing this information.

Since a strategic—a corporate investor—could later become an acquirer, there are some sensitive issues to be aware of. Allowing them to serve as the lead investor means they could end up with double-digit equity and a board seat. This could scare away other potential acquirers in the future when you're trying to set the stage for an acquisition exit. If these other suitors compete with your lead investor, they will realize the acquisition competition won't be on an even playing field. As a result, many startups try to keep such strategic investors to single-digit equity percentages and without special control or governance rights. Of course, all of this is balanced with the possible benefits the corporate investor can bring to help accelerate the growth of a great company.

COMMON ISSUES

The most common mistake I see founders make when raising a Series A is treating it like a larger version of a seed round but one that sells equity to investors rather than issuing them a convertible security. Boy, are these founders in for a surprise. Institutional investors evaluate different things during the dance, they have different expectations, and they operate in fundamentally different ways than angel investors. Remember that institutional investors are investing their limited partners' money, not their own. A Series A is far from just a larger version of a seed round.

If you are having difficulty securing a lead investor, you need to determine what the issues and inhibitors are. Hopefully, the investors themselves will tell you. If not, ask them what they would need to see in order for them to be excited about leading your Series A. If they give you a piece of feedback, ask if there is anything else they would need to see. This way, you get what's hopefully a complete list. Compare your lists from multiple investor conversations to see whether you can determine what is wrong. Following are the most common inhibitors to securing a Series A term sheet.

NOT ENOUGH BUSINESS PLAN VALIDATION

In the very beginning, your business plan was nothing more than a long list of assumptions. How many of those assumptions have now been validated? Are they the ones that demonstrate viability and at least hint at scalability? Each item in your business plan that gets validated either reduces the risks to the investor's investment or offers them more upside return potential.

NOT ENOUGH EVIDENCE OF TRACTION

For most tech startups, the form of traction Series A investors look for is an accelerating rate of new users or customers. They want to see a repeatable customer acquisition model. This translates to lots of associated traction metrics and unit economics that support your claims of customer acquisition proficiency. For a B2B startup, this might include trends for customer acquisition cost (CAC), CAC payback, average deal size, average sales cycle, and the like. For a mobile app startup using self-service acquisition, it might include trends for downloads, daily active users, conversion rates to a paid version, or perhaps ratios of advertising clicks—basically, any operational metrics that are key to customer acquisition.

Some startups have a longer path to customer acquisition and revenue. Examples include biotech and medical device companies. Series A investors for those segments will look for a completely different set of traction that relates to working prototypes, scientific validation, and milestone progress toward patents or regulatory approvals.

A SUBPAR TEAM

No doubt, the investors will sense your level of passion and determination. But remember that Series A venture funds are investing other people's money, and those people don't care about you or your passion. They just want to get a huge return on investment (ROI) due to the huge risk with this category of investment. The investors have no choice but to assess whether you and your co-founders are the ones to get the business venture to the next significant level. If not, it doesn't mean they won't invest, but it does mean they will need to have a discussion about bringing in some experienced executives. And that could also include a CEO replacement, with the founding CEO either remaining or not remaining in the company. This is when you must ask yourself how important it is to be rich versus the king or queen.

AN IMMATURE MANAGEMENT SYSTEM

When the company only has a couple of founders, there is no management system. But as employees are hired, results are generated, and projects initiated, the company will need some form of management system. You won't be expected to have an advanced and scalable set of processes and policies like a big company does, but you will be expected to describe how you set strategy, how you go about making important decisions, and how you manage the various company functions.

SUMMARIZING STARTUP SUCCESS

A Series A round of funding represents one of the most significant milestones for an early-stage venture, on par with launching the product and gaining the first paying customers. However, there are far more Series A fundable companies than there are venture funds to invest in them. Therefore, achieving this milestone is hugely validating. It also represents such a large injection of capital into the business that the gear shift is dramatically felt by all involved. If you've ever been in a high-performance sports car as it accelerated full speed from a standstill, it's sorta like that.

The cadence for a Series A funding round can be characterized as before the term sheet versus after the term sheet. Leading up to the term sheet, magic best happens when multiple lead investors present term sheets in a similar time frame. This offers you not only the best negotiating leverage possible but also the ability to select the investor you and your co-founders feel can best help grow a great company. I cannot overemphasize this point. Series A capital is not all the same shade of green. The right lead investor can be absolutely instrumental to your future success. So don't get greedy, and don't get caught up in distractions over nuanced investment terms. If you have a choice of investors and the terms are reasonable and broadly similar, go with the one that can best help you grow into a great company.

The due diligence performed by Series A investors will be much more professional than you experienced during the seed stage. You will not be able to hide important glitches or blunders—the investors will find them. The slopes of curves for your various trended results and KPIs really matter. They suggest a story that you will either boast or need to defend. And it is only fair that Series A investors perform this level of scrutiny. They are investing other people's money, and those people expect an outsized return on investment versus investing in real estate or the stock market.

 AHA MOMENTS

1. Investment decisions are made by partners and general partners of the fund.

2. Interested lead investors for a Series A propose their terms via a term sheet.

3. Some Series A investors only serve as lead investors, some only follow, and others will serve in either role.

4. Term sheets are perishable and usually only valid for two to three days. Following any negotiations, the term sheet is executed by both parties.

5. After executing a term sheet, the company is held to confidentiality via a *no shop* clause that typically lasts for 30 to 60 days.

6. An organized data room is the best way to share information for investor due diligence, both before and after a signed term sheet.

7. Series A rounds don't offer the flexibility of a rolling close but, rather, have a coordinated close that only happens once a certain required amount is committed by investors. If you don't reach that amount, you don't get your hands on new capital.

8. The Series A lead usually plays a role in helping close the rest of the round. This requires some coordination and regular communication with them.

9. An oversubscription allowance allows the company to raise more money than the minimum required amount and might be accompanied by a second or final closing of the round.

10. Corporate venture capital can operate similarly to or differently from traditional VCs. It is important to discover the investment thesis for each to determine if synergies exist.

CHAPTER 8

INTERACTING WITH INVESTORS

"It's not the size of the dog in the fight;
it's the size of the fight in the dog."

—Mark Twain

I often say that successful early-stage fundraising is essentially a transfer of enthusiasm from founder to investor. This is an adaptation of a mantra I learned a long time ago while in an enterprise sales role. But it's also true for fundraising. If the investor gets even half as excited as you are about the venture you're working on, their investment decision is already pointed strongly in your favor. So, let's evaluate some methods of transferring enthusiasm.

Each individual investor and venture fund is different in the way they like to interact during their investment evaluation. This difference is pronounced among angel investors and less so for institutional investors. But in either case, understanding the expected amount of time needed and the type of research to be conducted is hugely helpful to your planning and forecasting. It is disappointing when you think you've got several investors lined up together, only to later realize some of them were merely halfway through their decision process.

While interacting with investor prospects, the key is to find out how they go about making their investment decisions, in terms of both time and research. Below are some example questions to use:

- Which aspects of a business plan do you typically like to dive deeper into?

- What is your typical timeline and process for making investment decisions?

- How much time do you typically like to spend with a company before making an investment decision?

Some investors want to allocate extra time to evaluating the business model, while others want to dive deep into the product offering. Some want to spend a lot of time with the executive team to see how they interact with each other, while others prefer to deeply dissect the financial forecast model. Some angel investors can make an investment decision in a single, one-hour meeting, while others have a methodical, step-by-step approach that involves multiple meetings over a month or more.

As for when to ask the questions, it depends. I wouldn't spend valuable time during a short introductory meeting asking these questions, because you mostly want to develop rapport with the investor. Instead, if the intro meeting goes well, schedule a longer follow-up to get into more details. During the follow-up meeting, ask the first question (noted earlier) towards the beginning of the meeting so that you can optimize your time on the best topics. In fact, you can precede the question with something like "In order to make the best use of our time together . . ." Ask one of the time frame or process-related questions towards the end of the meeting to understand how things might play out going forward. After the meeting, write down what you learned so that you don't accidentally mix the investors up. You're going to meet a lot of them before closing your round.

Here's another trick. If you want to find out how an investor goes about making investment decisions, talk to other companies they have already invested in, just like doing a reference check on an employee prospect. And if the investor finds out you're checking up on them, they should actually be impressed. I would be.

INVESTORS WRITE CHECKS FOR OUTCOMES

During your interactions with investors, you will surely inform them how much you're raising. With that, you might get the obvious follow-up question: "Why is that the right amount to raise?" It's a very simple and justifiable question for the investor to ask, but it is commonly met with a host of unacceptable responses, such as the amount of runway it affords, the number of employees that can be hired, or the amount of dilution the founders are willing to tolerate. I even hear startups answer this question by saying that most other startups they talked to raised that same amount of money when they were at the same stage.

To every one of those answers, my response is: "So what? Why do I care?"

What investors want to know is what are the resulting strategic milestones and outcomes the funding will allow you to reach that will help secure viability (elimination of risks, increased traction, important validated learning, etc.), keep you on your path to achieving the stated vision, and eventually lead to an exit event that will give the investor a significant return on their investment. If staying on that path requires a lead architect, an inside sales rep, and some marketing activities, that's great. But don't put the cart before the horse. Your answers to "So what? Why do I care?" should become your explanations for why a specific amount of money is the right amount to raise.

You might have to ask yourself *so what?* multiple times in succession to get to the real answer. Below is an example:

Q: Why is that the right amount to raise?
A: It allows us to hire both a dedicated sales rep and a market development rep.

Q: So what? Why do I care?
A: Because the founders used to do all of the sales, and we haven't yet been able to launch our next geographic markets for our online marketplace.

Q: So what? Why do I care?
A: With these new resources, we can land our next 60 paying customers, reach $35,000 in monthly recurring revenue (MRR), and activate our next three geographic markets, all in the next 12 months.

BINGO!

Investors write checks for outcomes, not activities, and these are great examples of outcomes that can be achieved with the desired funding. You'll rarely get scrutinized if your newly acquired capital will be used to acquire a bunch of customers, open new markets, launch new sources of revenue, secure strategic partnerships, dramatically improve KPIs, and the like. So, rather than tell the investor how you are going to *spend* their money, instead tell them what you're going to *accomplish* with it.

This doesn't mean your planned activities and expenditures aren't important. We call them the *use of proceeds*. The investor might ask how you plan to acquire those next 60 paying customers and what your market activation playbook looks like. That's your chance—and obligation—to dive into the key activities that will enable you to accomplish the expected outcomes.

The concept is simple. Investors don't care as much about how you plan to use their money as they do about what you expect to accomplish with their money in your pursuit of an eventual great exit. So crack open your business plan to figure out what investors are really going to get for their money and communicate with them in those terms.

QUESTIONS TO EXPECT FROM INVESTORS

We just covered one question to expect from investors—why your proposed target funding amount is the right amount to raise. What other questions should you be ready for? The full list is very long and includes many obvious questions that you'll intuitively be prepared for. Let's skip those and instead cover 10 important questions you should be prepared for, regardless of your funding stage. If you haven't yet launched your product, substitute phrases like *How do you* with *How will you.*

WHY ARE YOU AND YOUR CO-FOUNDERS THE RIGHT ONES TO LEAD THIS VENTURE?

Of course you are smart and are hugely dedicated to your mission, so consider that table stakes. Did one or more of you suffer directly from the problem you're solving and are, therefore, on a passionate mission to solve it? Do any of you have relevant experience in your industry or technology focus area? Have any of the founders already built great companies or experienced exits that made investors a lot of money? These are examples of unique team attributes investors like to bet on.

HOW DO YOU ACQUIRE CUSTOMERS?

Take the investor on a journey through your customer acquisition strategy. What methods do you use? Which have proven to be most successful? What is the average cycle time for the buyer's journey? What are your important customer-acquisition-related KPIs, and how have they improved over time? Investors love it when they sense a well-oiled customer acquisition machine.

HOW DO YOU MAKE MONEY?

On the surface, this is a very simple question that ties to your pricing or monetization strategy. But why just tell the investor you have two subscription offerings at $399 and $999 per month? You have an opportunity to impress them with your understanding of your monetization strategy. Things like relative sales mix across your product line, rates of upsell or cross-sell, conversion rates from freemium to paid, and information about gross profit margins all add color and dimension to your response. What interesting insights can you share about your pricing and monetization strategy?

IS THE MARKET LARGE ENOUGH?

This might be a trick question. The investor knows you have already sized your market, but they want to see if you understand that size isn't everything. What else is it about your market that makes it ideal for growing a great company? Is it dynamic and undergoing massive transformation? Is the subsegment you're focused on growing rapidly? Is it highly fragmented and available for entry or dominated by a small number of behemoths? When asked this question, start with obligatory responses about the size of your market (TAM, SAM, beachhead) and then paint a more complete picture with additional favorable anecdotes.

WHAT EVIDENCE DO YOU HAVE THAT THE MARKET DESPERATELY NEEDS YOUR PRODUCT?

The key word in this question is *evidence*. A ton of paying customers is obviously direct evidence, but without that, you will need to draw from the massive amount of customer discovery and related research you conducted before you started building your product, as well as the additional interactions you had with customers during the beta-testing phase. Do your customers desperately *need* your product or just *want* it? There's a big difference. You desperately need oxygen to breathe. You want tickets to a popular band's upcoming concert. Those two things are not nearly of equal importance.

WHAT ARE YOUR MOST IMPORTANT KEY PERFORMANCE INDICATORS AND WHY?

The investor wants to confirm that you understand the underpinnings of your business across multiple functions. Are you hungry for insights and analytics to help fine-tune towards an optimized operation? Do you understand the metrics you track, the impact they have, and the relative interactions among them? An executive team that thinks and operates this way is one that can best adjust and adapt until a great company eventually results.

WHAT UNFAIR ADVANTAGES DO YOU HAVE?

Having the lowest price or the best user experience is not an unfair advantage. It's not that they are unimportant or invaluable, but they are rather short-lived advantages—not unfair ones. A really strong patent filing and access to proprietary data are examples of unfair advantages, assets your competition doesn't—and can't—have. It's actually possible that you don't have any truly unfair advantages over your competition. Many startups don't. But if you have some special sauce that nobody else has figured out, this question gives you an opportunity to boast.

WHAT IS YOUR BURN RATE?

Early-stage, high-growth ventures are consumers of cash. The question about your burn rate doesn't just inform investors about your available runway and associated cash fume date (the date you forecast running out of cash); it is a test to see whether you know what the question means. Many founders answer this question with their total monthly expenditures. But if you generate more gross profit than your expenditures, you are not burning cash; you're generating it. Your burn rate is the net difference between gross profit collected and expenditures. In other words, how much does your bank account balance go down each month? In addition to a test of your knowledge, this question is less about having a right versus wrong answer and more about the investor's need to understand your net cash consumption coming into the funding round.

HOW ARE YOU GOING TO REACH
$100 MILLION IN REVENUE?

The sum of $100 million is a nice, big, round number but also an interesting one. It's big enough to take several years or longer to reach, and that requires you to communicate the expected evolution of the company over that same period. It might require launching additional product lines, opening up international markets, or even making some acquisitions. A Series A investor likely needs you to reach something in the range of $100 million in revenue in order to be able to exit at a valuation that will yield them a tenfold or greater return on their investment. They want to make sure you aren't thinking only about surviving to the next round of funding, but rather getting your venture across an eventual goal line that makes everyone a lot of money.

WHAT IS YOUR EXIT STRATEGY?

This is another possible trick question. You want the investor to conclude that you're building a company that will eventually exit for a huge amount of money rather than one that will quickly sell out to an interested suitor after reaching only a few million dollars in revenue. If you answer the question with a list of six companies you've already identified as likely acquirers, you might come across as having an itchy trigger finger. Instead, first message that your focus is on building a world-class company with high growth, because they have infinite options over the long haul, including exits. If pressed for more specifics about who might acquire you, instead of reciting six specific companies, talk about the market or industry categories that have huge companies that are likely acquirers. With this backdrop established, you can mention a couple of specific company names, if they aren't already obvious.

INSIGHTS FOR UNDERREPRESENTED FOUNDERS

It is a disappointment—but not a secret—that the venture-investing world is full of white males. At the time of writing this book, this dynamic is changing, but so extremely slowly that it's hardly measurable. I, myself, am a middle-aged white male, so I can only pretend to know what it is like to be an underrepresented fundraiser sitting across the table from one or more white male investors. But a book on early-stage fundraising doesn't seem complete to me without acknowledging some unique issues those founders encounter as the chief fundraiser. For this, I'm only able to draw from what I've observed and learned as an advisor to numerous such founders.

Much of the issue has to do with cognitive bias, whether known or unknown, on behalf of the investor. For example, many male investors treat female fundraisers differently than their male counterparts. Part of this is reflected in the way they ask questions. They may ask all—or almost all—questions to a male co-founder that's also in the meeting. Or they may ask certain questions in a fundamentally different manner than they would to a male founder—in a way that tends to put the female founder on the defensive rather than framed around the vision and upside potential of the investment opportunity. In fact, the title of an article published in the *Academy of Management Journal* in 2018 summarizes this point perfectly: "We ask men to win and women not to lose."

Continuing with the female fundraiser example, one best practice I've observed is to answer certain biased questions first with information that conveys the long-term vision, upside potential, and evolution of a great company. After that, it's possible that additional information needs to be conveyed so as to answer the direct question asked. Here is an example:

Q: Why won't you collapse under your own weight as you continue expanding your marketplace to new geographic markets? A: Expanding to the top 10 markets in the US alone will bring our serviceable market up to $650 million. We are already profitable in our home market and are posting 30% month-over-month growth. Our new market activation playbook has been in use for two months in our second market, and all of our assumptions have been validated so far. In fact, let me show you our KPI dashboard to give you some additional insights.

A natural tendency might be to answer the direct question by going into defensive mode. The example response shown does the opposite. It's not an answer to a totally different question, similar to what most politicians do all the time. Instead, it starts by framing the company's mid-range potential ($650 million SAM), then discusses some current success (already profitable in the home market and with 30% monthly growth), and finishes with something more directly related to the question but framed in a positive context (new market activation playbook already in use and working well). Offering to dive into some metrics is just icing on the cake.

Similar issues of cognitive bias surely exist when the chief fund raiser is a founder of color, an immigrant founder, an LGBTQ founder, disabled, or an elderly founder with wrinkles and gray hair. Until the cross-section of venture investors looks much more like a cross-section of our society, this issue will continue to persist at some level. If you are an underrepresented founder, find others like you who have been successful in their fundraising endeavors. They can advise you much better than I can on this issue that, unfortunately and undoubtedly, you will face at some level and frequency—hopefully diminishing over time.

QUESTIONS TO ASK SERIES A INVESTORS

The investors aren't the only ones that get to ask questions to assess the investment opportunity. You get to do the same, and you should. Your relationship with investors will last a long time, and that means going through several ups and downs together on your way to an eventual exit. You need investors that will be supportive in a variety of ways. This mostly relates to institutional investors rather than angels that invested during the seed stage. Institutional investors take seats on your board of directors, they often invest across multiple rounds of funding, they help you find the best investors for rounds of funding after that, and they have a huge voice (and, sometimes, contractual rights) in key business decisions.

Perform your own due diligence on Series A investors, especially any that you're considering to be the lead investor. Do so by asking your advisors about their reputation. Better yet, talk to executives at other startups they invested in. Try to get specific examples of how they've been supportive. In addition, ask the investor various questions to get specific information and insights into how they operate. Following are some examples to consider asking during the multiple interactions you will have with them over time. In other words, don't whip out the full list of questions during the introductory meeting.

WHAT MAKES AN IDEAL INVESTMENT FOR YOUR FIRM?

Each venture fund has an investment thesis that influences their investment decisions. It is usually some combination of company stage, industry, business model, and technology. In other words, one fund might focus on Series A startups with enterprise software, while another might focus on late-seed and Series A startups with solutions for the healthcare industry. The funds make this pretty easy to figure out by just reading their website and looking at their existing investment portfolio. But ask some questions to dive a little deeper and identify any important nuances or new areas of focus. The answer to this question will probably also include mention of typical investment amounts and target equity amounts.

HOW WOULD YOU DESCRIBE YOUR CURRENT FUND?

Most venture funds have a 10-year lifecycle that starts with a few years for making new investments followed by several years to make follow-on investments into those same companies. After asking this question, you should expect the investor to describe the size of the fund they are currently making new investments from, when the fund first started investing, the number of investments they've made, and the total number of companies they are likely to invest in from the fund. You might also get a chronology of their prior funds.

DO YOU PROVIDE BRIDGE FINANCING, AND DO YOU INVEST ACROSS MULTIPLE ROUNDS?

If the fund reserves a certain amount for follow-on investments, it can be used for short-term bridge rounds or the next equity round of funding. Try to find out how much they typically reserve and what forms of funding it can be used for. Ideally, the answer will include some actual examples within their portfolio. If the fund doesn't reserve for follow-on investments, ask how they help their portfolio companies secure future rounds of funding.

HOW DO YOU LIKE TO ADD VALUE FOR YOUR PORTFOLIO COMPANIES?

This is a nice, open-ended question that can have a wide range of responses, and it's mostly for the lead investor. For each expression of added value, try to get an example. Are you hearing things that you agree are hugely valuable based on your current team's skills, the stage of the company, and the issues and opportunities you are facing?

WHAT IS YOUR BACKGROUND?

This question is mostly for the partner or GP that will sit on your board of directors, which also means it's a question for prospective lead investors. Board directors serve in both an oversight and an advisory capacity. Ideally, the investor representative that sits on your board will bring some unique value that complements the other board members. Investors that previously had a successful career as an operator will bring different perspectives than the ones that entered the venture world right after getting an Ivy League MBA. Neither is bad or good; they're just different. What skills and experience would benefit you the most?

COULD YOU INTRODUCE ME TO ONE OF YOUR PORTFOLIO COMPANIES THAT YOU FEEL IS MOST LIKE US?

Investors will be happy to brag about their successful companies, but what you want is to talk to a couple of their portfolio companies that have some resemblance to yours. If your founders are first-timers, seek a similar company. Or maybe the resemblance will relate to your monthly revenue, business model, or product type. The more similarities, the better, but realize that the venture fund might have only a couple dozen portfolio companies in total, so you might not find a perfect match.

EVIDENCING TRACTION

Traction is a very special attribute when it comes to fundraising and is something investors will want to learn a lot about during your interactions. It trumps almost any other form of evidence you might have that your business is worth investing in. Think about it. It you have a bunch of paying customers, the investor might not fully agree with your customer acquisition strategy, pricing model, or competitive comparison, but they've got to give you credit for having real, paying customers. For this reason, if you have that most genuine form of traction (paying customers), you should diplomatically flaunt it. If you don't have it, everything else you do will mostly be hand waving to distract from the fact that you don't have that form of traction.

If you don't yet have paying customers, don't give up. Instead, get creative on your definition of *traction*. To my way of thinking, traction can be just about anything that serves as evidence of desirability (the market wants it) and business model viability. Work your way backwards from paying customers to identify the closest thing you do have. Below is a list that does just that. If you want to improve your answer to the investors' traction inquiry, do things to progressively move your way up the list.

- Paying customers
- Firm orders that haven't yet been fulfilled by your company

- Firm orders that are contingent on something being completed first (successful trial, needed feature, needed certification, and the like)

- Paid trial

- Signed nonbinding letters of intent to order (signed by an executive is much better than signed by a first-level manager)

- Verbal intentions to order

- Freemium or free trial

Your list might be different based on your business model. But if you find yourself lower on the list than desired or if your business is of the type to not generate revenue for quite some time (e.g., it involves deep science or requires regulatory approvals), it's time to get even more creative. Remembering my definition of *traction* (evidence of desirability and viability), identify other things that can serve as some level of validation. Below are some examples to broaden the aperture of possibilities:

- Acceptance into a credible startup accelerator

- Milestones reached towards eventual regulatory certification

- Experienced and reputable advisor joins your advisory board

- Experienced employees agree to work for no cash compensation

- Letter of intent (or better) with a prospective distributor or strategic partner

- Relevant award or similar recognition
- Favorable review by a notable industry influencer

All of these accomplishments involve someone scrutinizing your business potential. As such, they at least offer hints of desirability or viability. If you don't have any such accomplishments, go get some, and include them in your traction narrative until something more significant from the first traction list serves as a replacement.

EVIDENCING TRACTION THROUGH ENTERPRISE TRIALS

In the list above, you noticed that we included free trials and paid trials as possible ways to evidence traction. But not all trials are alike in this regard. Startups with a self-service business model and a low-cost solution won't get much traction credit from their free trial customers but rather from evidence that leads to monetization. That could be conversions to the paid product version, clicks that result in advertising revenue, or accumulation of data that is somehow monetized.

That's not the case with startups that sell to large enterprise organizations, because very few sales happen in that environment without the customer first conducting a trial. Just securing a trial with a large enterprise is unbelievably difficult, because the implications of failure are exaggerated. Just imagine what it takes to get a hardware or software product installed in the main data center of Walmart or Bank of America. Large enterprises have a fairly regimented process before deciding to purchase a product for wide-scale rollout. Successfully making it through just the first steps of their process is validating to the point of evidencing traction to investors. If you sell to large enterprises, you need to understand a few things in order to get full traction credit from investors when you secure trials.

WHAT'S IN A NAME?

I've used the word *trial* up to this point, but you will also see words like *pilot* and *proof of concept (POC)* used to describe a prospective customer taking your product out for a test-drive as part of their purchase evaluation. Is there any difference between these descriptions? Actually, there is—even though you might hear many people use them interchangeably.

Proof of concept

Typically lasting 30 to 60 days, a POC is performed by the prospective customer in a controlled, nonproduction environment (e.g., a lab). It is intended to verify the functionality they were shown during demonstrations and to confirm interoperability, compliance, and other basic fundamentals before exposing the product to real users.

There are several nuances to keep in mind for using POCs to gain traction credit. First, who gave the verbal commitment or signed the letter of intent? This person is your project champion. The more senior their title, the better a champion they'll be for your pursuit of closing a real deal. If your project champion is also the decision-maker for an eventual purchase, even better.

Your investors will also weight your traction credit on the basis of competition for POCs. If the POC involves one or more competitors, it suggests that you haven't yet convinced the customer you are the best alternative to solving their stated problem. But if the POC is with you alone, it is more validating and will gain you more credit.

If the POC involves one or more competitors, it is unlikely the customer will be willing to pay anything. But if you are being considered in isolation, it might be possible to get the customer to pay for the POC. A monetary investment—of any amount—for your POC is evidence of traction. The fact that you convinced Walmart to pay to test your product is hugely validating—and not easy to accomplish.

Hopefully you understand the criteria the enterprise will use to decide whether your product is worthy of moving to the trial stage. If so, and if you already have evidence of meeting the criteria, you can use that for credit. And if you are already in discussion about purchase intent (for a trial or larger), that's even better. If you were able to get a conditional purchase order before starting the POC, that's badass.

Trial or pilot

Although some people give different definitions to the words *trial* and *pilot*, I see them as mostly synonymous. They are performed in a production environment, which is one key difference between them and a POC. The other key difference is that real users are involved, but on a limited basis. Perhaps the trial is performed only with a specific department or in a single geographic location. The functionality might also be limited in scope.

A trial is not usually performed unless the enterprise has decided to purchase the product. However, it is possible that a shaky trial will prevent a broad rollout and even kill the deal completely. There is no typical duration for a trial. It lasts long enough for the enterprise to fully validate their intent for a broad rollout and to develop plans to do so.

Using trials as evidence of traction entails some nuances. For example, it is not uncommon to negotiate special pricing for a trial deployment (i.e., deeper discounts than normal). But if you can get the customer to pay a reasonably discounted price, you can get credit with investors. I usually try to negotiate the pricing for a large (even global) deployment and agree to use that same price for the trial, as long as the customer provides good faith intent to proceed with the larger deployment if the trial is successful.

The size, extent, and duration of the trial may also affect the level of traction credit you get. The larger the trial (more users), the better, and the more extensive the use of the product (more functionality), the better. However, a longer trial phase means a later and more uncertain expanded rollout. Since you don't get extra credit for the length of a trial, work with your customer to define the most efficient but extensive trial possible, and prepare to devote the resources to ensure it stays on a successful track.

INCREASING YOUR LEVEL OF TRACTION CREDIT

It's clear that investors will give you full and undisputed credit for a satisfied enterprise customer that has paid for and deployed your product on a global scale. But between a verbal commitment for a POC and that global rollout are lots of milestones that deliver increasing credit.

Based on the definitions provided earlier, a trial is obviously more credit-worthy than a POC. But don't underestimate the significance of successfully starting a POC with a large enterprise organization. They don't deploy their resources and infrastructure without considerable thought and planning. Just navigating that successfully offers some validation to your business plan. Even just getting a signed letter of intent (LOI) to start a POC carries some validation.

In figure 8.1, you can see that, within each of these forms of enterprise engagement, there are increasing degrees of traction credit to achieve. Progressing as far to the right as possible will earn you maximum credit with investors. Find the best mix of quantity (number of simultaneous trials underway) and quality (pushing as far to the right of the graphic above as possible). But even that's not sufficient if you don't message properly to investors. Think about your strategy ahead of time so that you can set goals accordingly and come up with the right plan of attack.

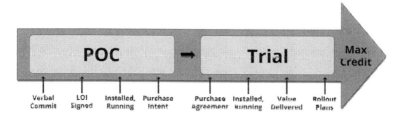

Figure 8.1. Evolution of a POC and trial

ASPIRATIONS, EXAGGERATIONS, AND OUTRIGHT LIES

Most startup founders don't realize how bad they are at predicting the future, how far they stretch their claims, and how much refactoring investors have to do as a result. During your interaction with investors, you must progressively earn their respect and generate credibility. You will need to do so while still coming across as hugely driven, passionate, and absolutely unstoppable.

The most successful entrepreneurs thrive in the face of perpetual chaos and skepticism. They have unmatched survival strengths and are regularly told to "fake it until you make it." All of this is just the reality of the early days of building a great company. The issue comes down to the parallel need to earn both respect and credibility from other stakeholders that will ultimately determine the success of the venture—investors being a significant example.

ASPIRATIONS

In the early days, startups have lots of aspirations. As I just said, your initial business plan is a huge list of assumptions. Most of those assumptions are actually aspirations that need to be true in order for your proposed business plan to hang together without a big pivot.

My friend and Capital Factory business partner, Joshua Baer, often recommends that founders forecast to investors when they are going to accomplish certain things and then just go do exactly that. Maybe it relates to launching your product, acquiring a certain number of new customers, or securing an important partnership. Josh stresses that it's so difficult for startups to predict the future that just doing what they said they were going to do is hugely impressive to investors. Here's an easy one to start with: Tell interested investors you're going to send them monthly company updates. Then do it like clockwork for minor credibility boosts every time.

Prototypical startups are off-the-charts optimistic and often run by first-time founders that are either just starting or early in their business career. Because of this, their forecasts (aspirations) are way too aggressive and optimistic. I'm not talking about their long-term vision and potential, but rather their predictions of what will happen in the next 90 days, and especially in the next 12 months.

Most active investors are experienced pattern matchers. They've interacted with hundreds of startups, which means they've heard hundreds of forecasts and predictions. Since 90% of them aren't achieved, it's no surprise that investors automatically give them a haircut without even thinking about it. I know what you're thinking: "We're not like every other startup." It's totally possible that you are a member of the 10% club, but you're going to have to prove it first.

Your first step is to look backwards at your history of accomplishing what you said you were going to do. Look back at the prior goals and forecasts you and your co-founders wrote down. How many of them did you fully accomplish? In the range of 50% is probably typical, 20% to 30% is concerning, and 70% or greater is impressive. I'm mostly talking about the prelaunch and early revenue phases of the company, when you're still trying to develop a well-oiled machine. The bar obviously gets much higher as you approach the sweet spot for a Series A.

If your prior track record is favorable, great. If not, you need to quickly get to work on improving it so you can demonstrate to investors that you're a member of the elite 10% that accomplishes what they say they will. To do this, you need to understand that there are two key elements of the equation:

PREDICTION

Foretelling the future is extremely difficult, especially for a startup venture. It takes practice and a learned ability to figure out which inputs to weigh greater than others. The evolution of your business (customers, competitors, employees, etc.) means the types and quantities of inputs are regularly changing. This further complicates things, because it's as if the rules are always changing. It seems that way because they are.

EXECUTION

When you saw the future in the crystal ball, you made assumptions about your team's ability to execute their respective roles in order to accomplish the stated goals. But by doing so, you just made three key assumptions: You assumed you're capable of communicating the goals in such a way that they are well understood. You assumed your team is able to perform their required tasks, both as individuals and as a coordinated team. And you assumed you are able to quickly adjust and adapt if—or when—things don't play out as expected.

Unfortunately, you don't get credit for missing your predictions due to unforeseen circumstances. From the investor's perspective, the exercise is simple. You said you would accomplish X in time frame Y. Only one obvious question matters to your investor: Did you accomplish or exceed X within Y?

In the earliest days, you probably have part-time, volunteer, and third-party contributors to your efforts. That makes both prediction and execution even more difficult. Now you know why 90% of startups don't accomplish what they said they would, even over short periods of time.

The only way to get good at this is to build a culture of predicting, executing, measuring, refining, and repeating—again and again and again. This will pay dividends not only in the early days while you're trying to become a part of the 10% club but also in the future, when you set a goal of generating $50 million in annual revenue and becoming profitable.

EXAGGERATIONS

Just as investors apply a haircut to stated predictions until you demonstrate a track record of achieving them, they've unfortunately learned that it is best practice to do the same with your stated claims about what you have *already* accomplished. This is due to the regular exaggerations that many founders make. I know—not you. But let me first give some examples to see if you still feel the same.

Claim: "We have a product that does A, B, and C."
Reality: "We are actively building a product that will be able to do A, B, and C."

Claim: "We're currently at $25,000 in MRR."
Reality: "Last month, we recognized $25,000 in revenue. Of that, $15,000 was from subscription software, and $10,000 was from a one-off services project."

Claim: "We have an awesome team of five people."
Reality: "We have two full-timers, two part-timers, and one advisor."

Claim: "We've closed $300,000 of our $1 million seed round."
Reality: "For our $1 million seed round, we have $100,000 in the bank, $150,000 in verbal commits, and $50,000 in indications of interest."

Claim: "We already have 10 customers."
Reality: "We gave six of our original beta customers free licenses for six months and have two paying customers and two late-stage trials that we expect to convert soon."

Surely you see where I'm coming from. Have you already communicated in this manner? The difference is reflected in words you use, like *have* and *closed*. It's only after the investor double-clicks for clarification that they discover what they conclude is an exaggeration. Sometimes, it's actually the omission of information that causes the perception of exaggerating.

What you have to decide is how far to push these exaggerations. The investors expect you to be aggressive, boastful, and proud. And you might not actually get penalized for minor exaggerations here and there. But if you were to stack up all five of the claims made above, you're going to have a huge credibility problem on your hands. And that's a negative hit to the desired enthusiasm transfer I talked about. At a minimum, it means continued haircuts to every claim you make rather than gradually earned credibility. And in the worst case, it causes the investor to cease their investment consideration.

OUTRIGHT LIES

Like exaggerations, outright lies are discovered as investors dig deeper into your claims. They result either from something you think is a slight exaggeration but the investor begs to differ or from the way you answer their questions. Let's use the example claim above about already having 10 customers. If the investor asks, "Are they actual paying customers?" you have a choice. You can answer the way the reality statement was worded above, or you can say "Eight of the ten are paying customers." That would be an outright lie, because six of them have a free license.

Eyeing a cash fume date that's just around the corner can cause us to do crazy things that we would never do in more normal situations. But it's not just your cash fume date that can cause these misjudgments in ethics. Desperately wanting to show that you accomplished what you said you would or being in the final push to get a funding round closed can offer the same tempting risk. Don't do it!

Getting caught in an outright lie crosses an important line for many investors. If you'll lie about one thing, why not many more things throughout the future of the company? Building trust with your stakeholders (not just investors) is paramount to being able to call on them during very difficult times to help bail you out of a mess. The same is true for asking them to open their contact list to make a key introduction; they won't do that if they don't trust you. The negative ways that lying can impact you are infinite.

Nothing described here should cause you to be less bold, driven, confident, passionate, or unstoppable. Those personality traits are 100% compatible with building a well-oiled machine that is able to predict the future, achieve it, and do so with strong ethics and hugely loyal stakeholders.

SUMMARIZING STARTUP SUCCESS

Fundamentally, the process of fundraising is analogous to the process of sales. Both involve an offering, a set of features and associated benefits, and an agreed economic value exchange. Both also involve interactions between humans, which means relationships are established, debates are common, and credibility must ultimately be earned if the result is to be successful. When I described successful fundraising as a transfer of enthusiasm, I didn't just mean having a contagious smile on your face or a spring in your step. Of course, those things are required. But it also requires earning credibility with the investor over time and across multiple dimensions.

Just like selling a product, each customer cares about different things and goes about making decisions in different ways. In sales training, we are taught how to identify these attributes so that we can best navigate a successful sales process. It's the same with fundraising, but with investors as the customer. Being prepared for common questions and answering them in ways that both inform and help transfer enthusiasm are key to your success.

If you haven't already, you will soon realize your pre- and post-traction periods translate to very different conversations with

investors. Before you have the best form of traction (paying customers), you need to get creative with alternate ways to evidence it
but without too much exaggeration and definitely without lying.
Once you do have paying customers, this issue will be behind you
but replaced with interrogation about metrics, trends, and customer acquisition proficiency. Like I said before, growing a great
company never gets easy. Rather, it remains hard but in different
ways over time. That doesn't mean it can't be hugely rewarding and
fun; it usually is.

 AHA MOMENTS

1. Successful early-stage fundraising is essentially a transfer of
   enthusiasm from founder to investor.

2. Ask questions to discover how a given investor prefers to
   go about making their investment decisions. This includes
   the type of information needed and the process they like
   to follow.

3. Investors write checks for outcomes, not activities. First
   message what you plan to accomplish with the new funding
   (outcomes). When asked how you plan to accomplish those
   things, inform about your tactical plans for spending the
   money (activities).

4. Be prepared with answers to the 10 most common questions investors will ask.

5. When evaluating a prospective Series A lead investor, make
   sure to do some interviewing of your own.

6. Cognitive bias is a behavior most investors exhibit, even unintentionally. If you are not a white male, you likely will experience it during your face-to-face investor interactions. Understanding the most common biases and seeking insights from like founders can help you improve your odds of fundraising success.

7. There are numerous forms of potential traction evidence leading up to paying customers. If something suggests evidence of desirability (the market wants it) and business model viability, investors might be willing to treat it as traction. Get creative.

8. Convincing a large enterprise to test-drive your product is not easy and, therefore, is validating. They usually start with a POC in a controlled environment and, if successful, perform a trial or pilot in a production environment but with limited scope.

9. Accomplishing what you foretell you will do is a way to earn credibility with investors, but it's harder to do than most founders think—even over short periods of time and especially in the very early days before operational maturity is developed.

10. Excessive exaggerations are a way to wipe away any earned credibility and enthusiasm, and getting caught lying is an outright deal killer.

CHAPTER 9

NEGOTIATING VALUATION

"That which does not kill me makes me stronger."

—Friedrich Nietzsche,
German philosopher and poet

I once heard an experienced investor use the phrase "Tell me your price, and I'll tell you my terms." It stuck with me, and I've since applied it to a variety of key business negotiations, such as technology licensing, mergers and acquisitions, and of course fundraising. It uniquely captures the fact that a fair deal for both parties involves a combination of something that resembles price and a whole host of legal rights and terms. For a round of funding, the *price* is the valuation of the company seeking investment. It is so often the most negotiated item in a round of funding that it is worthy of a dedicated chapter.

Founders often get so infatuated with the amount of dilution they're going to experience as a result of taking on new funding that they focus almost exclusively on getting the highest valuation possible. I've even seen founders practically fall on their swords in order to eke out a $7.7 million pre-money valuation instead of the investor's proposed $7.5 million. Come on! Really?

DEFINITION: PRE-MONEY AND POST-MONEY VALUATION

Since the injection of new capital into a company immediately increases its value, we use the terms *pre-money* valuation and *post-money* valuation to help explain the difference. As seen in figure 9.1 and excluding a few exceptional situations, the post-money valuation is the pre-money valuation plus the newly raised capital. The shorter slang terms *pre* and *post* are often used to designate which version of valuation is being referring to.

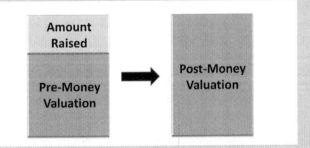

Figure 9.1.

A key significance of the post-money valuation is that it determines how much equity an investor will get. In other words, if the negotiated pre-money valuation is $4 million and an investor invests $1 million, they will end up with 20% equity. That's because the post-money valuation is $5 million, and $1 million as a percentage of $5 million is 20%.

You will probably hear the mantra: "Time kills deals." It means that in the extra time it takes to convince the investor to nudge up to the desired $7.7 million valuation, a couple of things can happen. They could drop your deal in exchange for another one or, to the point made before, they could insert other terms into the term sheet or edit existing ones in such a way that the higher valuation is offset in a different way. The offset might not be reflected in purely financial terms but rather could involve control terms like board seats, voting rights, or blocking rights. You either just lost an investor or effectively ended up right back where you started in terms of balance in the offer.

DEFINITION: LIQUIDATION PREFERENCE

A liquidation preference is a typical right affiliated with preferred stock that is sold to investors. It ensures that the investor gets paid first in the event the company is sold at a distressed value. Until the preferred shareholders get their invested amount back, other shareholders (i.e., holders of common stock) don't get paid. In fact, preferred shareholders with this right get to choose between whatever is better—getting their liquidation preference or getting their relative equity percentage of the total acquisition price. The liquidation preference is expressed as a multiple of the investor's invested capital. A 100% payback preference is typical (investors might refer to it as a 1X liquidation preference).

HOW INVESTORS THINK ABOUT VALUATION

Investors use a combination of art and science to either evaluate the valuation you propose to them (if using convertible securities) or determine the valuation they will propose to you (equity rounds of funding). If you find yourself discussing valuation, it is mostly a good sign. That's because investors don't focus too much on valuation until they've learned enough to decide whether they have some interest in investing in the first place. If they determine they have interest, much of the information they discovered during their evaluation goes into an assessment of a reasonable valuation.

It's probably obvious that each investor has their own approach to assessing valuation. This is especially the case with angel investors. But when it comes to institutional investors, family offices, and highly disciplined angels, I've found there is a common sequence of events that typically occurs behind the curtain.

COMPARABLES

Active investors see tons of deals. This means that, after completing their initial evaluation, they are able to pattern match your opportunity with several others. They have an ability to compare various aspects of your business plan and strategy to magically match it up with prior deals they invested in, ones they decided to decline, and ones they lost to other lead investors. They are essentially identifying other deals like yours and their associated valuation. This evaluation of comparables gives them a general starting point for valuation.

"Deals like yours" means other companies with similar levels of traction, similar team skills and track record, and similar market size. It might also mean companies in the same industry or with the same business model. These are the key attributes of your business plan and business opportunity, so it's logical that they also serve as the basis for identifying similar prior investments and their associated valuation. Investors won't be able to make an exact match, but they try to get as close as possible with this part of their assessment.

ADJUSTMENTS

Since the pattern matching exercise surely didn't result in an exact match to other recent deals they felt had a fair valuation, the investor will make some adjustments. During their initial evaluation, they likely discovered some things that especially impressed them or especially concerned them. These become additions or subtractions from their starting valuation. Maybe you have a superstar on the founding team or have already landed a significant strategic partnership. Those would serve as valuation boosters. Or maybe you had a recent pivot that's not yet proven or an excessively high churn rate. Those would be valuation subtractors.

TARGET EQUITY TEST

Many institutional investors have a target equity amount they need to get when they invest. In fact, some investors have a fairly strict and narrow equity target, whereas others have a more flexible and general rule of thumb. If their target is 18% to 22% and their valuation assessment to this point would result in them only getting 15%, they will likely reduce their proposed valuation to get their equity back into the target range. You might be wondering why they can't just invest more money to reach their target. They can; you just have to convince them to do that instead.

POTENTIAL EXIT RETURNS

Early-stage investors take much more risk than those that invest during later stages. As a result, they often make investment decisions based on the likelihood of getting at least a tenfold return (you might hear investors refer to it as a 10X return). So the next step in their process involves running various exit scenarios. With this, they are trying to answer a very specific question: What valuation would you need to be acquired for (or go public for) in order to give them a tenfold return? To run this calculation, they also need to make some assumptions about the number of future rounds of funding you will need to raise and how much dilution they will experience from each. But the formula is based on simple algebra that you will see in figure 9.2.

$$\frac{10 * \text{Initial Investment}}{\text{Initial Equity} * \text{Aggregate Dilution Until Exit}}$$

Figure 9.2. Investor tenfold-return formula

If we assume two future rounds of dilutive funding, the formula would look like figure 9.3.

$$\frac{10 * \text{Initial Investment}}{\text{Initial Equity} * \text{Dilution Factor 1} * \text{Dilution Factor 2}}$$

Figure 9.3. Formula for two future rounds of funding

Regarding dilution, my personal rule of thumb is to expect 25% to 35% dilution with each *real* round of funding. Equity rounds of funding are typically real rounds, but bridge rounds aren't. Bridges usually dilute less than average if they are truly just to bridge a gap.

What many founders ignore or forget is the dilutive effect of funding rounds in which convertible securities are used. A seed round that is raised on convertible notes will also dilute 25% to 35%. It's just that the dilution isn't experienced until the notes actually convert to equity. That results in what feels like a double whack of dilution, but it's really just two rounds of funding over time with the dilution from both experienced at the same time. For example, a seed round using convertible notes that is 30% dilutive followed later by a Series A that is also 30% dilutive will feel like 51% total dilution (0.7 * 0.7 = 0.49) at the time the notes convert to equity. It's as if anesthesia from the seed round eventually wears off with the Series A and the full brunt of the dilution is experienced at the same time.

Let's run the exit return calculation for an investor whose $2 million investment yields them 20% initial equity, and let's assume two more rounds of funding that are each 30% dilutive before an eventual exit. Perhaps this is an investor in your Series A round, and they assume you will need to raise both a Series B and Series C in the future before becoming profitable and sustainable. The calculation is as follows:

$$(10 * \$2 \text{ million}) \div (0.2 * 0.7 * 0.7) = \$204 \text{ million}$$

Using the assumptions in this scenario, the company needs to exit at a valuation in the range of $200 million in order for the investor to get a tenfold return on their investment. We don't cover mergers and acquisitions in this book, but I can tell you that a typical high-growth company needs in the range of $40 million to $60 million to achieve that sort of exit valuation. Now the investor's assessment is clearer. What are the odds your company can both successfully grow to approximately $50 million in annual revenue and find an acquirer willing to pay $200 million?

You will notice that the initial equity amount is expressed in decimal form (20% = 0.2). The dilution factors are also expressed in decimal form, but we have to determine the inverse percentage first. That is why 30% dilution is expressed as 0.7. This is the same concept as trying to figure out how much a $60 pair of shoes will cost with a 10% discount. We multiply $60 * 0.9 to get the discounted price of $54.

Now, rerun the calculation with some variations the investor will be thinking about. What if they agree to some higher valuation and have to invest $3 million to get their target equity? (The new answer is $306 million.) What if a third round of future funding is needed to reach the eventual exit? (The answer is $292 million.) What if the future funding rounds dilute only 20%, or perhaps worse at 35%? (The answers are $156 million and $237 million, respectively.) What if each of the prior worst-case scenarios are combined? (You'd need a $546 million exit valuation.)

It seems logical to me that this hypothetical investor will assess the odds that your company can reach an exit somewhere in the range of $200 million to $300 million and will also be thinking about the possibility that the exit might need to reach $500 million or more. Hopefully, now you understand why professional investors seek businesses that can grow to the point of being able to exit for hundreds of millions of dollars and not just tens of millions. You additionally should conclude that the investor will be thinking about the evolution of the company all the way to an exit and not just the next round of funding. You must be of this same mindset.

DEATH RISKS

A final sanity check the investors might conduct is an assessment of death risks—of the startup, not your founding team! All startup ventures are inherently risky, but some have either discretely identifiable or excessive risk of death before reaching an exit. An example is a required regulatory certification in order to be able to sell the product commercially. If the certification is not granted, the startup is likely to die or be sold in distress. Another example is publicized hints from an industry giant that they are considering bringing a product to market that would be directly competitive with your startup's. Remember that investors need to see a path all the way to an exit that gives them a tenfold return. Excessive death risks will factor into their valuation assessment because early-stage investments are mostly about the risk-reward trade-off.

THE DIFFERENCE WITH ANGEL INVESTORS

Some of the steps outlined here also apply to angel investors, who typically invest in pre-seed and seed rounds of funding. First, they aren't typically as methodical in their assessment of valuation. As such, they might rely mostly on comparables and adjustments. Angels that are more active might also calculate the potential exit return, but even they don't usually have a target equity amount like some venture funds do.

Neither institutional nor angel investors precisely follow the chronological methodology described here for assessing valuation, starting with comparables all the way through death risks. But that doesn't mean forcing yourself to walk through these same steps with the investor's hat on is a waste of time. You will be far more prepared than almost all first-time fundraisers, and even many experienced fundraisers, when it comes time to negotiate your valuation.

TIME TO NEGOTIATE

Since the valuation you're able to negotiate is such a key aspect to your funding round, why not go ahead and go through the same steps the investors go through? Find other recently funded companies that look like you—similar funding, amount of traction, stage, market size, experience among the founding team, and so on. What sort of valuations were they able to negotiate? What positive and negative adjustments can you identify as likely? Can you immediately start working on any of the negative adjustments? Can you quickly add more positive adjustments?

For the VCs you are building relationships with, do they have a target equity amount and, if so, what is it? You probably won't find this information on their website but might be able to talk to some founders in their portfolio or founders that pitched them but didn't get a term sheet. Maybe your advisors know the answer or could find out. Actually, during your second or third meeting with a venture fund, you can probably just ask them directly. It is not a taboo question if the interactions to that point have been positive and they seem generally interested.

What sort of future exit will you need in order for your prospective investor to get a tenfold return with the valuation you're hoping for? You've got the formula. Run various scenario calculations before the investor does.

ANCHORING THE DESIRED VALUATION

During any negotiation in which the price is not already known, the two negotiating parties have a choice of who utters a suggested amount first. Which is the best approach to take? Well, you can find lots of articles and books on negotiation that explain the pros and cons of anchoring the conversation. The first suggested or offered figure creates a cognitive bias that causes the other party to more heavily rely on that initial piece of offered information. If the buyer goes first, they usually suggest a lower number than they are actually willing to pay. If, instead, the seller starts the negotiation, they will do so with a number higher than they are truly willing to accept.

If the investor anchors the conversation by suggesting a $4 million pre-money valuation and then, through discussions and more evaluation, decides to come up to $4.5 million, you might have the feeling that it is a good deal. Although the outcome is the same, the experience is different than if they started with $4.5 million and remained firm on that number.

Don't assume you can be the one to first anchor the conversation at an $8 million valuation in hopes that negotiating down to $4.5 million will leave the investor feeling like they got a great deal. Your mention of a valuation that seems ridiculously high can quickly terminate the investor's evaluation. You've got to at least be within a reasonable range.

I don't have a single recommendation in regard to who mentions valuation first, because every situation is different. I do believe you should decide on a range of valuations you think is reasonable and would be acceptable to you and your key stakeholders. And if you did your homework during the planning phases of your fundraising campaign by having penalty-free conversations with investors before officially launching the campaign, you should have gained some valuable insights about the acceptable valuation range.

AFTER THE TERM SHEET FROM A LEAD INVESTOR

Let's say a prospective lead investor gives you a term sheet that includes reasonable terms in general but the valuation is measurably lower than you expected and also below the range you and your key stakeholders previously agreed would be acceptable. Now what?

Your first and most significant negotiating tool comes from having *alternatives*. Many negotiating articles and books talk about the importance of understanding what's called your BATNA (best alternative to a negotiated agreement). Do you have any other term sheets for a similar amount of funding? If not, are others likely to come soon? Are there alternative forms of funding available, such as grants or venture debt?

You could decide to raise less money to better match the valuation and yield reasonable dilution. If you do so, are there other likely investors that would be interested? Simply raising less money at the proposed lower valuation might yield an acceptable amount of dilution, but just make sure the outcomes you can achieve with this reduced funding will still be exciting in the future. If not, you might not get the needed step-up in valuation at that time. Worse, you might be on the fundraising trail again much sooner than desired.

Must you raise money now, or do you have an option to execute for at least a few more months before needing fresh funding? If you don't have other active investor prospects but do have some runway left, you could put your head down and execute like crazy while fixing some of the things that prevented you from getting the valuation you needed. Or maybe you've got some exciting milestone accomplishment coming soon that you can achieve first to help justify your desired valuation.

If you don't have one or more of these alternatives available, you are pretty much at the mercy of the single investor proposing a term sheet, and you'll need to use additional negotiating tools.

Your second negotiating tool comes from decoding the investor's evaluation of your company and debating anything that genuinely doesn't seem valid. Most likely, this involves finding out the concerns they had (valuation subtractors) and trying to convince them they shouldn't be as concerned. You will also want to make sure they are giving you credit for things you feel are deserved (valuation boosters). Just realize that there isn't any sort of price list that matches dollar amounts to these things. It's much more subjective than that.

Your third negotiating tool is to see whether there are other terms in the term sheet that you can trade for an increased valuation. This can get very dangerous, and you must first get the advice of an experienced attorney, because you could otherwise accidentally do great harm to your company.

Your fourth negotiating tool comes into play if the lead investor is only investing half or less of the total amount for the funding round. With this, you might be willing to offer them extra equity in exchange for a higher valuation. You do this outside of the direct investment, with an instrument like a warrant, which is an option to purchase shares in the future at today's price. The net result is that the lead investor will still get their target equity (or maybe close enough), and the other investors that fill in the rest of the round will invest at the higher, more desirable valuation. Even with the extra equity offered to the lead investor, you might come out better in terms of overall dilution. But you are also betting that other investors will gauge the valuation as acceptable. Instead, you could just be outpricing yourself for those other needed investors.

INVESTORS HAVE ALTERNATIVES TOO

It is possible that your desired valuation is completely reasonable, but it is a competitive market. Active investors have lots of alternatives. They might be considering other investments that have similar potential to yours but at a lower valuation. Your valuation is not assessed in isolation but, rather, among a list of opportunities the investor is considering.

THERE'S A TIME TO STOP ARGUING

You are only worth what investors will agree you are worth. Additionally, your mission is not to find the absolute highest valuation you can get from a single investor that will invest first. Instead, you need to find a valuation that lets you efficiently close your full round of funding so that you can get back to running your business.

There is an opportunity cost associated with getting greedy on the required valuation, and other key funding terms, for that matter. The longer it takes to close the funding round, the later the new resources are added and the longer you are spending 80% of your time in the grind. In the meantime, your business will suffer at least some impact. And the later you and the new resources are able to contribute to operational goals and objectives, the later the needed exciting outcomes are achieved. This ripple effect and associated opportunity cost are often either overlooked or underestimated.

If you find yourself arguing about valuation with all or most of the prospective investors, I'm sorry to say it, but your valuation is too high. You aren't worth as much as you thought. But if you are forced to reduce your valuation, it is not the end of the world. Find a good investment partner that can help you grow a great company. They are far more valuable than a mediocre one that will give you a slightly higher valuation. Your mission is to optimize for growth, not dilution.

THE DIFFERENCE WITH VALUATION CAPS

Convertible securities don't actually set the valuation of the company at the time of investment. But the valuation cap feature does put a high-side limit to the possible future valuation that will be used to determine how much equity the holder of the convertible security will get. Because of this, investors go through an evaluation of the proposed valuation cap amount in mostly the same manner as described previously. But there are some nuances that are worth understanding.

Convertible securities are not actually required to have a valuation cap. It is a protection mechanism that some startups are able to remove. Doing so means the sky is the limit for the future valuation when the security converts. The only economic reward the investor would get is their discount. Only startups in high demand for their investment round are able to get away with that. It is by far the exception, not the rule.

Proposing a reasonable valuation cap for your convertible security is as much art as science, since you probably don't have a long enough track record of results to produce pretty trend graphs and the like. Finding comparables of other startups that are like yours and recently raised a similar round of funding using a convertible security is a great way to start. You can then also evaluate reasonable adjustments that should be made, as described before. But to properly negotiate the valuation cap with an investor, you first have to think about their perspective versus yours for this important feature of convertible securities.

THE INVESTOR'S PERSPECTIVE

The investor wants the cap to be as low as possible so that their investment converts to as much equity as possible in the future.

When the cap comes into play, there is a good chance the effective discount will be higher, and possibly much higher, than the discount they were entitled to. For example, if a convertible note has a $5 million valuation cap and the pre-money valuation of the future equity investment that causes conversion is $7.5 million, a note holder will get an effective discount of 33.3%. That is significantly better than the typical 20% discount the investor was probably entitled to as a worst case.

Deep down inside, many investors know the cap is in place to protect them on the high side, should the startup grow like a rocket ship with their investment. But they must assign some probability that you will do just that. This means if you present them with a valuation cap they feel is high, they have to be comfortable with the possibility of converting to equity using that cap amount for the valuation.

Some investors don't really see the valuation cap as a protection mechanism, especially if the post-money version of the SAFE is being used. The post-money SAFE is structured in such a way that it begs both parties to approximate today's valuation via the cap amount. Investors that don't see the valuation cap as mostly a protection mechanism might tell you there's no way your company is worth that valuation today. In other words, they are trying to make the cap reflect your hypothetical valuation today, even though you're not officially setting the valuation for an equity round of funding today. To my way of thinking, a major justification for using convertible securities in the first place is because setting a valuation for the company at that time (usually very early stages) is nearly impossible.

THE STARTUP'S PERSPECTIVE

You'd love it if you didn't have to include a cap at all so that you have the possibility of driving a really high future valuation and minimizing dilution for yourself and your co-founders when the securities convert to equity. But since your opportunity isn't so hot that investors are giving you blank checks and begging to get into your deal, you have no choice but to include a valuation cap.

Or maybe you just fundamentally feel it's fair to include one. Startups tend to see the valuation cap only as a worst-case protection mechanism for the investors. If their investment allows you to grow like a rocket ship and to reach a crazy-high valuation for the future equity round that triggers the conversion to equity, the early investors absolutely deserve some protection and economic reward.

I can summarize the different perspectives this way: Investors want the valuation cap to come into play upon conversion so they can get a greater effective discount than the one they are entitled to, whereas startups want the valuation cap to solely be a protection mechanism with lower odds of coming into play.

DON'T FORGET THE DISCOUNT

Something investors commonly forget or ignore in the valuation debate is their entitled discount. The discount means the future valuation for the equity round can be higher than the cap amount and the investor will still convert at a valuation that is lower than the cap. Let's look at an example convertible note with a $4 million cap and a 20% discount. In this case, the investor only benefits from the cap if the company raises their future equity round at a pre-money valuation higher than $5 million (20% discount from $5 million = $4 million). This means any valuation lower than $5 million gives the investor exactly the same equity as if the note didn't have a cap at all.

I am purposefully using a convertible note example because of the calculation complexities with a post-money SAFE.

In case this is confusing, let's look at it a different way. Many entrepreneurs think that a $4 million cap means that any negotiated pre-money valuation higher than $4 million results in the cap coming into play. But because of the 20% discount, the cap doesn't come into play until the *discounted* equity valuation exceeds the cap. In this example, it means the future valuation must exceed $5 million before the cap comes into play. Any equity-round valuation lower than $5 million gets discounted 20% to a resulting number that is lower than the $4 million cap.

The scenarios described previously can be seen in figure 9.4.

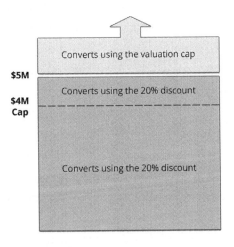

Figure 9.4. Conversion scenarios

Having demonstrated this, most investors will mentally evaluate the likelihood that their investment converts at the valuation cap amount versus the discount. It requires them to look into a crystal ball, but they do it anyway. In order for them to invest, they must be comfortable with the possibility of converting to equity using either scenario.

RESPONDING TO PUSHBACK

Let's get specific. A prospective investor says to you, "There's no way your company is worth $4 million today. Your valuation cap needs to be lower." Assuming you have reasons to believe your proposed valuation cap is fair, here's a possible response: "We are proposing a $4 million cap to protect our early investors in the event their investment allows us to skyrocket and raise an equity round in the future at a much higher valuation than normal. But remember that with your 20% discount, a $4 million valuation in the future would allow you to convert into equity at a $3.2 million valuation. We would actually need to reach a valuation higher than $5 million before this cap comes into play."

However, if most investors are telling you that your valuation cap is too high, then it probably is. Your only real alternative is to look at the other proposed terms for your convertible security to see if there is something you can change to offset the seemingly high valuation cap. Increasing the discount is probably the most logical choice, since it also relates to the economics of future equity conversion. But doing that also has future trade-offs for you and your existing shareholders.

Because of the numerous scenarios that could play out for the future conversion to equity, I recommend using a cap table simulator to forecast what the post–Series A cap table and various equity positions would look like after the convertible securities convert to equity. Run scenarios with different valuation caps and even see what the result looks like with a higher-than-normal discount. You should be armed with this information before negotiating the valuation cap with investors—because many of them will be.

SUMMARIZING STARTUP SUCCESS

If you reach the point of debating or negotiating valuation for your funding round, congratulations! You've made it a long way. That's because investors don't usually put much emphasis on valuation until they've decided they are legitimately interested in your opportunity. You don't take a new car out for a test-drive if you hate the style or it's missing features you consider critical. But lots of fish wiggle off the fundraising hook during the valuation negotiation step. It is a very important term to both parties, because it often carries the biggest long-term economic leverage for both.

Active investors, both angel and institutional, are savvy pattern matchers, and that can be a good thing or a bad thing for you. If the comparables they identify yield a favorable starting point for your valuation, great. But if you are so unique that they can't really think of a similar company, it might be hard for them to figure out what a reasonable valuation is. They take some comfort in having comparables as a starting point for their evaluation.

It is easy to get excited about the prospect of a nice, high valuation. But your mission is not to spend every last bit of time and energy to eke out every last bit of valuation. Time kills deals, and the longer you're on the fundraising trail, the longer your company is without your complete operational focus. If you find yourself arguing the valuation with every investor, your desired valuation is wrong. If, on the other hand, you have multiple highly interested investors, you probably have something to work with. Just don't try to get too fancy playing your poker hand. Instead, identify the investors that can best help you continue to grow a great company, get the funding round closed, and put your focus back on creating that great company. The only equity percentage that matters is the one you have when you eventually exit. And if you've built a great company by then, the super-huge exit multiplied by almost any equity percentage is still a huge number.

 AHA MOMENTS

1. "Tell me your price, and I'll tell you my terms." Seek a balanced deal.

2. When discussing valuation during an equity round of funding, make sure to be clear whether you're talking about pre- or post-money figures.

3. Investors use multiple methods to evaluate valuation. Use those same methods to make an assessment yourself.

4. Perform the exit return calculation using a range of assumptions for future funding rounds needed to reach an exit. This will inform you as to how big you need to grow in order for the investor to make a tenfold return on their investment.

5. Each real round of funding will likely dilute existing shareholders in the range of 25% to 35%, but variations outside this range certainly can happen for a variety of reasons.

6. Dilution from real rounds (not bridges) that use convertible securities won't be felt until they convert to equity, which has the compounding effect of the shareholders experiencing two rounds' worth of dilution at the same time.

7. Having alternatives, especially other investment offers, is possibly the best tool for negotiating valuation.

8. Optimize for growth, not dilution.

9. The valuation cap in a convertible security does not necessarily set the valuation for converting to equity in the future but rather represents one scenario. The other scenario results from the discount being utilized. The investor gets the more favorable of the two calculations.

10. If using a SAFE, make sure to confirm whether the template calls for a pre-money or a post-money valuation cap, because the difference to the future equity cap table can be meaningful.

CLOSING THOUGHTS

I hope the preceding chapters were both informative and enlightening enough to deliver numerous aha moments. I also hope
that this book will serve as a future reference tool each time you
make a decision to raise money out of want or need. If I caused you
to dog-ear lots of pages and highlight lots of sections that you want
to be able to quickly refer back to, I have accomplished a personal
goal. But as much as you might have learned from this book, please
don't underestimate the value of experienced mentors, advisors, corporate attorneys, and other entrepreneurs that have been through
the fundraising journey before. You want to seek and exploit all the
help you can get. And if their advice differs from what I've written
here, don't get frustrated. Instead, dig a little deeper to understand
why they are making the recommendation, and then decide if it
better resonates with your philosophies and your situation.

As much as it might seem like fresh funding will address most
of the things that are keeping you awake at night, I find that's not

usually the case. Fundraising is actually a distracting activity that occurs multiple times along the evolution of a high-growth venture. It is a necessary evil—a means to an end. It's not the closing of a round of funding that makes a founder or their company successful, but rather what they do with the combination of time and resources the funding affords them.

New funding serves as fuel for the fire and a flip of the hourglass that you don't want to run dry. But you still have to build a great company over time. That means hiring a great team, fostering a desirable company culture, maturing in ways that bring predictability to your results, forming the best strategic partnerships, getting really good at making important decisions, and eventually navigating a successful IPO or acquisition exit at the right time. I wonder if those topics would make for a good book. Hmm, interesting idea.

INDEX

A

acceleration of growth, Series A funding, 142–44
accelerators, startup, 55, 108
accountability, 2, 43
accredited investors, 54
adaptability, 24–25
amount to fundraise, deciding on, 45
  outcomes, 33–34
  overview, 31–32
  resources, 32–33
  runway, 32–33
  time, 32
  valuation, 35–37
anchoring valuation, 198–99
angel investors, 53, 54–57
  approach to valuation, 197
  defined, 16
asking for money. *See also* fundraising
asking for money phase, fundraising, 51–52, 64
aspirations, forecasting to investors, 180–81
assumptive metrics, 24–25

B

backup section, pitch decks, 84–85
Baer, Joshua, 180
BATNA (best alternative to a negotiated agreement), 200
bootstrapping
  assumptions, 13–14

benefits of, 9–10
dilution, 9–10
for how long, 11–13
mindset, 13
overview, 8–9
bridge rounds, 22, 27
  convertible securities as, 113–14, 118
  questioning investors about, 171
  valuation and, 194–95
burn rate, 166
business models
  pitch decks, 80–81
  pre-seed funding, 61
business plan, seed-funded startup, 17

C

CAC (customer acquisition cost), 12, 154
calling the note, 107
call to action, pitch decks, 83–84
campaign phases, fundraising
  allocating appropriate time for, 64, 65
  asking for money, 51–52, 64
  cash fume date, 51
  determining investor interest, 49–50, 64
  preparation and prioritization, 50–51, 64
  prioritized list of investors, 51
cap, convertible securities, 102–6, 115, 117, 203–5, 210

capitalization table (cap table), 38, 104, 139

capitalization table simulators, 38, 106, 207

cash fume date, 51, 166

CEOs, 49, 65, 154–55

change of control, defined, 105

chief fundraiser, 48–49, 65

Churchill, Winston, 29

closing round
  initial close, 149
  rolling close
    convertible securities, 113, 116
    seed funding, 133
  second close, 149
  seed funding, 126–28
  Series A funding, 148–49, 157

cognitive bias of investors, 168–70, 187

common stock, 100, 101

comparables, evaluating, 192–93

confidence monitor, 94

convertible notes, 106–12
  defined, 106
  flexibility of, 112–13
  interest rate, 107–8
  qualified financing, 108
  SAFE securities compared to, 108–12
  term, 107

convertible securities, 99–118
  benefits of, 114–15
  as bridge round, 113–14, 118
  convertible notes, 106–12
  discount, 101–2, 114–15, 117
  flexibility of, 116
  overview, 99–101
  rolling close, 113
  SAFE securities, 117
  term, 114
  valuation cap, 102–6, 115, 117, 203
    early exit multiple, 105–6
    overview, 102–3
    simulating future equity conversion, 106

corporate venture capital (CVC), 149–52, 157

Crossing the Chasm (Moore), 40

crowdfunding, 53

current funds, questioning investors about, 171

customer acquisition cost (CAC), 12, 154

customers
  questions from investors about, 164
  target customers for pre-seed funding, 60–61

CVC (corporate venture capital), 149–52, 157

D

data room, 139–40, 150–51, 157

da Vinci, Leonardo, 99

death risks, investors' evaluation of, 197

deceleration of growth, Series A funding, 142–44

desirability, 11, 15–16, 173–74, 187. See also traction

dilution, 27
  dangers of optimizing for, 38–39, 45
  defined, 9–10
  valuation and, 194–95, 200, 209

discount, convertible securities, 101–2, 114–15, 117, 205–7

due diligence, 148, 150, 156, 170–73

E

early exit multiple, 105–6

Edison, Thomas, 7

Eisenhower, Dwight, 47

elevator pitch, 68–74, 97
  brevity, 69
  conversational tone, 71
  explaining why it's important, 70–71
  overview, 68–69
  practicing, 72–73
  simplicity, 71–72
  summarizing venture, 69–70
  varying for audience, 73–74

employees, seed-funded startup, 17–18

enterprise trials, evidencing traction to investors through, 175–78

overview, 175–76
pilot, 177–78
POC, 176–79
equity dilution, 27
equity rounds. *See also* seed funding;
    Series A funding
defined, 19
rolling close, 113
valuation and, 192, 194–95, 205–6,
    209
exaggerating, when forecasting to inves-
    tors, 182–84
exit returns, investors' evaluation of,
    193–96
exit strategy, questions from investors
    about, 167

F

family/friends funding, 9
family office, defined, 55
feasibility of startup, 11, 15
Feld, Brad, 148
final close (second close) funding target,
    149
financial projection model, 94–95, 98
first close (initial close) funding target,
    149
flexibility
    of convertible notes, 112–13
    of convertible securities, 116
    of startup, 24–25
flow, pitch decks
    backup section, 84–85
    business model, 80–81
    call to action, 83–84
    explaining problem to be solved,
        76–78
    market, 78–79
    solution, 79–80
    summary, 85–86
    team, 82–83
    traction, 82
Ford, Henry, 119
forecasting to investors, 179–85, 187

aspirations, 180–81
exaggerations, 182–84
executing goals, 181–82
lies, 184–85
predictions, 181
Formica, Michael, 68
foundation, pitch decks, 75
founders
    bootstrapping, 9
    choosing when to fundraise, 2
    handling questions from investors,
        163–67
    optimizing for growth, 38–39
    questions to ask potential investors,
        170–73
    seed-funded startup, 17–18
    underrepresented founders, 168–70
freemiums, 81, 95
fundraising
    accountability, 2, 43
    bootstrapping, 8–14
        assumptions, 13–14
        benefits of, 9–10
        for how long, 11–13
        mindset, 13
        overview, 8–9
    capitalization table simulators, 38
    crossing fundraising chasm, 40–43
        bridge rounds, 42–43
        overview, 40–41
        planning multiple seed rounds, 42
        raising larger seed round, 41
    deciding how much to raise, 31–39,
        45
        outcomes, 33–34
        overview, 31–32
        runway, 32–33
        valuation, 35–37
    dilution, 38–39
    fear and, 3–4
    idea phase, 14–15
    multiple funding rounds, 37
    need-versus-want situation, 29–30
    planning
        campaign phases, 49–52, 64–65
        chief fundraiser, 48–49, 65

hyper-intersected angel investors, 66
    prospective investors, 53–57
pre-seed funding, 14–17, 53–54
    business models, 61
    challenges, 58–59
    hyper-intersected angel investors, 59
    industry, 60
    product category, 61
    target customers, 60–61
    technology, 61–63
reasons for, 2
science of, 39
seed funding, 17–18
    closing phase, 126–28
    hitting wall/plateau, 128–31, 134
    messaging scarcity factor, 134
    middle phase, 124–26
    rolling close, 119–20, 133
    securing early investors, 120–24
    verbal commitments, 134
self-funding, 8
Series A funding, 14–15, 18–20
    common inhibitors to securing,
        153–55
    CVC, 149–52, 157
    due diligence, 148, 150, 156
    financial projections, 95
    information sharing, 139–40, 157
    investors, questions to ask, 170–73
    overview, 135–37
    term sheets, 136, 137–39, 147–49,
        155–57
    trended metrics, 140–46
tools
    elevator pitch, 68–74, 97
    financial projection model, 94–95,
        98
    overview, 67
    pitch decks, 74–88, 97–98
    pitching events, 88–94
fundraising chasm, crossing, 40–43
    bridge rounds, 42–43
    overview, 40–41
    planning multiple seed rounds, 42
    raising larger seed round, 41

G

gear shifts, startup, 21
government grants, 53
GPs (general partners), 138, 152
Gretzky, Wayne, 135
grind phase, seed funding. See middle
    phase, seed funding
growth trajectories, Series A funding,
    144

H

headcount, personnel, 33
HVPP (hope, vision, promise, and
    potential), 16–17
hyper-intersected angel investors, 59, 66

I

idea phase, 14–15
industry, investors' knowledge of, 60
information sharing, Series A funding,
    139–40, 157
initial close (first close) funding target,
    149
interest rate, convertible notes, 107–8
investment thesis, questioning investors
    about, 170–71
investors, 53–57. See also Series A
    funding
    angel investors, 16, 53–57, 197
    approach to valuation, 192–97
        adjustments, 193
        angel investors, 197
        comparables, 192–93
        death risks, 197
        potential exit returns, 193–96
        target equity test, 193
    cognitive bias of, 168–70, 187
    determining investor interest, 49–50,
        64
    developing rapport with, 160–61
    differences between, 159–60
    evidencing traction to, 173–79, 187

increasing level of traction credit, 178–79
overview, 173–75
through enterprise trials, 175–78
finding, 56–57
focus on outcomes, 161–63, 186
forecasting to, 179–85, 187
aspirations, 180–81
exaggerations, 182–84
executing goals, 181–82
lies, 184–85
predictions, 181
hyper-intersected angels, 66
networking, 57
pre-seed funding, 53–54, 58–63
business models, 61
challenges, 58–59
hyper-intersected angel investors, 59
industry, 60
product category, 61
target customers, 60–61
technology, 61–63
prioritized list of, 51
questions to ask, 170–73
about added value, 172
about background, 172
about bridge financing, 171
about current fund, 171
about investing across multiple rounds, 171
about investment thesis, 170–71
about similar portfolio companies, 172–73
questions to expect from, 163–67
about burn rate, 166
about customers, 164
about exit strategy, 167
about founders, 164
about KPIs, 165–66
about market, 165
about monetization strategy, 164
about probability of reaching $100 revenue, 167
about unfair advantages, 166
evidence for product viability, 165
overview, 163

seed funding, 54–55, 120
favorable terms, 121–22
motivating, 126
overview, 120–21
progress updates for, 125
tracking, 125
verbal commitments, 122–24
tenfold return formula, 194
transfer of enthusiasm to, 159, 185

J

judges, pitching events, 93

K

Keynote pitch presentation, 90
KPIs (key performance indicators), 18, 165–66

L

lead investors, Series A funding, 135–37, 156–57. *See also* term sheets, Series A funding
leapfrog opportunities, 22–23
letter of intent (LOI), 178
lifetime value (LTV), 12
limited liability company (LLC), 111
liquidation preference, 191
LOI (letter of intent), 178
LTV (lifetime value), 12
lying, when forecasting to investors, 184–85

M

market
pitch decks, 78–79
questions from investors about, 165
SAM, 78
TAM, 78–79

maturity date
  convertible notes, 107
  convertible securities, 114
Mendelson, Jason, 148
middle phase, seed funding, 124–26
  attitude during, 125
  motivating investors, 126
  progress updates for investors, 125
  tracking investors, 125
mindset, bootstrapping, 13
minimum viable product. *See* MVP
mock pitches, 92
monetization strategy, questions from
  investors about, 164
Moore, Geoffrey, 40
multiple funding rounds, 37
MVP (minimum viable product)
  pre-seed funded startup, 15
  seed-funded startup, 17

N

need-versus-want situation, 29–30
Nietzsche, Friedrich, 189
no shop clause, term sheets, 147, 157

O

$100 million revenue goal
  growing startup to, 145–46
  questions from investors about, 167
one-page executive summary (one-
  pager), 96–97
onstage version
  pitch decks, 86–87
  pitching events, 88–89
operational metrics, 95
opportunity cost, 202
optimizing for growth, 38–39
optimizing reward, 58
optimizing risk, 58
outcomes
  investors' focus on, 161–63, 186

role in deciding how much to fundraise, 33–34
oversubscription, Series A funding, 149,
  157

P

P&L (profit and loss), 95
partners, 138, 152
PDF pitch presentation, 90
pitch decks, 97–98
  defined, 74
  flow, 76–86
    backup section, 84–85
    business model, 80–81
    call to action, 83–84
    explaining problem to be solved,
      76–78
    market, 78–79
    solution, 79–80
    summary, 85–86
    team, 82–83
    traction, 82
  foundation, 75
  onstage version, 86–87
  practicing, 87–88
  simplicity, 86
  sit-down version, 86–87
pitching events, 88–94
  day of presentation, 93–94
  judges, 93
  memorization, 89–90
  overview, 88–89
  practicing, 92
  preparation for, 89
  presentation formats, 90
  Q&A session, 92–93
  slides, 91
pivots, 21, 24, 27, 41
planning fundraising
  campaign phases
    allocating appropriate time for, 64,
      65
    asking for money, 51–52, 64
    cash fume date, 51

determining investor interest,
    49–50, 64
preparation and prioritization,
    50–51, 64
prioritized list of investors, 51
chief fundraiser, 48–49, 65
hyper-intersected angel investors, 66
overview, 47–48
prospective investors, 53–57
    finding, 56–57
    networking, 57
    for pre-seed funding stage, 53–54,
        58–63
    for seed funding stage, 54–55
    for Series A funding stage, 55–56
POC (proof of concept), 176–79
portfolio companies, questioning inves-
    tors about, 172–73
post-money valuation, 190–91
PowerPoint pitch presentation, 90
predictions, forecasting to investors, 181
preferred shares, 100, 101
pre-money valuation, 190–91
pre-seed funding
    investors, 53–54
        business models, 61
        challenges, 58–59
        hyper-intersected angel investors, 59
        industry, 60
        product category, 61
        target customers, 60–61
        technology, 61–63
    P&L, 95
    phases of, 14–17
presentation formats, pitching events,
    90
priced rounds. See equity rounds
product category, pre-seed funding, 61
product viability, questions from inves-
    tors about, 165
profit and loss (P&L), 95
proof of concept (POC), 176–79
prospective investors. See investors

Q

Q&A session, pitching events, 92–93
qualified financing (qualifying transac-
    tions), convertible notes, 108
questions to ask investors, 170–73
    about added value, 172
    about background, 172
    about bridge financing, 171
    about current fund, 171
    about investing across multiple
        rounds, 171
    about investment thesis, 170–71
    about similar portfolio companies,
        172–73
questions to expect from investors,
    163–67
    about burn rate, 166
    about customers, 164
    about evidence for product viability,
        165
    about exit strategy, 167
    about founders, 164
    about KPIs, 165–66
    about market, 165
    about monetization strategy, 164
    about probability of reaching $100
        revenue, 167
    about unfair advantages, 166
    overview, 163

R

RBF (revenue-based funding), 99
risk-reward tolerance, 34
ROI (return on investment), Series A
    funding, 154
rolling close
    convertible securities, 113, 116
    seed funding, 133
runway, 2, 32–33, 44, 56

S

SAFE (simple agreement for future equity) securities, 108–12, 117, 204
SAM (serviceable market), 78
scarcity factor, messaging, 127, 134, 148
second close (final close) funding target, 149
SEC (Securities and Exchange Commission), 53, 54
seed funding, 17–18
  closing phase, 126–28
  hitting wall/plateau, 128–31, 134
  messaging scarcity factor, 134
  middle phase, 124–26
    attitude during, 125
    motivating investors, 126
    progress updates for investors, 125
    tracking investors, 125
  rolling close, 119–20, 133
  securing early investors, 120–24
    favorable terms, 121–22
    overview, 120–21
    verbal commitments, 122–24
  verbal commitments, 134
self-funding, 8
Seneca, 67
Series A funding, 14–15, 18–20, 135–57
  CVC, 149–52, 157
  due diligence, 148, 150, 156
  financial projections, 95
  information sharing, 139–40, 157
  inhibitors to securing, 153–55
    immature management system, 155
    insufficient business plan validation, 153
    insufficient evidence of traction, 154
    subpar team, 154–55
  overview, 135–37
  questions for investors, 170–73
  term sheets, 137–39, 155–56
    closing round and, 148–49, 157
    defined, 136
    negotiation process, 147–48

    no shop clause, 147, 157
    oversubscription, 149, 157
  trended metrics, 140–46
    acceleration versus deceleration, 142–44
    growing to $100 million, 145–46
    growth trajectories, 144
    overview, 140–41
    slope of curve, 141–42
serviceable market (SAM), 78
Silicon Valley investors, 34, 45
simple agreement for future equity (SAFE) securities, 108–12, 117, 204
sit-down version, pitch decks, 86–87
slides, pitching events, 91
solutions, pitch decks, 79–80
spinning flywheel metaphor, 19–20
staggered discount, convertible securities, 115
startups
  bridge rounds, 22
  gear shifts, 21
  leapfrog opportunities, 22–23
  measuring success, 1–2
  optimizing for time, 2–3
  overview, 20–21
  pivots, 20–21
storytelling, pitch decks, 76–78
strategics, 150, 152

T

TAM (total available market), 78–79
target customers, pre-seed funding, 60–61
target equity test, 193
team, pitch decks, 82–83
technology, pre-seed funding, 61–63
tenfold return formula, 194
term
  convertible notes, 107
  convertible securities, 114
term sheets, Series A funding, 137–39, 155–56

closing round and, 148–49, 157
defined, 136
negotiation process, 147–48
no shop clause, 147, 157
oversubscription, 149, 157
using when negotiating valuation,
    199–200
tools, fundraising
  elevator pitch, 68–74, 97
    brevity, 69
    conversational tone, 71
    explaining why it's important,
        70–71
    overview, 68–69
    practicing, 72–73
    simplicity, 71–72
    summarizing venture, 69–70
    varying for audience, 73–74
  financial projection model, 94–95, 98
  overview, 67
  pitch decks, 97–98
    defined, 74
    flow, 76–86
    foundation, 75
    multiple versions, 86–87
    practicing, 87–88
  pitching events, 88–94
    day of presentation, 93–94
    judges, 93
    memorization, 89–90
    overview, 88–89
    practicing, 92
    preparation, 89
    preparing for Q&A session, 92–93
    presentation formats, 90
    slides, 91
topic order, pitch decks. See flow, pitch
    decks
total available market (TAM), 78–79
traction
  evidencing to investors, 173–79, 187
    increasing level of traction credit,
        178–79
    overview, 173–75
    through enterprise trials, 175–78
  pitch decks, 82

Trafton, Mikey, 69–70
trended metrics, Series A funding,
    140–46
  acceleration versus deceleration,
      142–44
  growing to $100 million, 145–46
  growth trajectories, 144
  overview, 140–41
  slope of curve, 141–42
Twain, Mark, 69, 159
2X multiple, 106

U

uncapped convertible securities, 105
unfair advantages, questions from inves-
    tors about, 166
unit economics, 18, 81, 154
use of proceeds, 163

V

valuation
  defined, 35–36
  dilution and, 194–95, 200, 209
  discount and, 205–7
  handling pushback, 207–8
  influence of, 36–37
  investors' approach to, 192–97, 209
    adjustments, 193
    angel investors, 197
    comparables, 192–93
    death risks, 197
    potential exit returns, 193–96
    target equity test, 193
  liquidation preference, 191
  negotiating, 198–202
    anchoring valuation, 198–99
    using alternatives, 200–201
    valuation boosters, 201
    valuation subtractors, 201
    warrants, 201
  opportunity cost, 202

overview, 189–90
post-money valuation, 190–91
pre-money valuation, 190–91
valuation boosters, 201
valuation subtractors, 201
valuation cap, convertible securities,
        102–6, 115, 117, 203–5, 210
$3.5 million valuation, 103
$4.5 million valuation, 104
$6 million valuation, 104–5
early exit multiple, 105–6
overview, 102–3
simulating future equity conversion,
        106
VCs (venture capitalists), 142–43
Venture Deals (Feld and Mendelson),
        148
venture funds, 55

verbal commitments, seed funding, 134
viability, startup
   defined, 12
   MVP, 15
   questions from investors about, 165

W

warrants, 201

Y

Y Combinator (YC) accelerator, 108

ABOUT THE AUTHOR

GORDON DAUGHERTY is a seasoned business executive, entrepreneur, startup advisor, and investor. A proud native Texan, Gordon grew up in a small town and graduated from Baylor University with a computer science degree. He spent the first 10 years of his career in brand-name companies such as IBM and Compaq and then progressively gravitated towards early-stage and high-growth companies. Gordon spent eight years in the videoconferencing industry, including four years as president of an Israeli company that grew from $5 million to $36 million in a short few years and went public on the Euronext Stock Market.

Gordon oversaw most company functions while serving in executive capacities, but his primary focus was on strategy, marketing, sales, business development, and M&A. He was a senior executive for Austin-based NetQoS, which grew rapidly to more than $55 million in revenue before being acquired by CA Technologies for $200 million, and he was a founding advisor for digital advertising pioneer MediaMind, which reached $65 million in revenue and a NASDAQ IPO in 2010.

Gordon has vast experience with early-stage fundraising from both sides of the table. As a venture fund manager and angel investor, he has made more than 200 investments. He has also helped raise more than $80 million in growth and venture capital as a company executive, fund manager, board director, and active advisor.

Through his content creation practice, Shockwave Innovations, and as co-founder and president of Austin's Capital Factory, Gordon now spends 100 percent of his time educating, advising, and investing in tech startups. He serves on the board of directors for several Austin-based technology companies and is a managing director at SoftMatch, a corporate innovation advisory firm.

Over the years, Gordon has given personal advice to several hundred entrepreneurs, and more than 1,000 startup founders have completed his Founders Academy boot camp. He has published more than 150 startup advice articles and is the producer of a video library with 50 streaming titles of educational content for startup founders.

Now having raised three daughters, Gordon and his wife of more than 25 years enjoy spending time at their beach house on the Texas coast or at some global destination they've never been before.

Made in the USA
Middletown, DE
12 January 2020